For my Parents
Henrietta May Hastie (1924 – 2001)
Kevin Wordworth Edwards (1929 – 2005)
In Love, Respect and Gratitude

A Sprinkling of Magic

How to Captivate your Audience with Inspiring Stories and Metaphors that give Meaning to your Message

3rd Edition – April 2025

Practically Positive Publishing
© 2025 Clare Edwards

Limit of Liability and Disclaimer of Warranty

The author has used her best efforts in preparing this book and the information provided herein is provided 'as is'. Practically Positive Publishing makes no representation or warranties with respect to the accuracy or completeness of the contents of this book and specifically disclaims any implied warranties of merchantability or fitness for any particular purpose and shall in no event be liable for any loss of profit or any other commercial damage, including but not limited to special, incidental, consequential, or other damages.

Where references are made to third parties, permission has been sought to include their information and contact details have been provided where appropriate. No remuneration has been sought for citing these parties.

No part of this document or the related files may be reproduced or transmitted in any form, by any means (electronic, photocopying, recording, or otherwise) without the prior written permission of the author.

Images used in this book have been sourced and purchased from multiple royalty-free sources and the author's personal picture collection.

A Sprinkling of Magic

Contents

LIMIT OF LIABILITY AND DISCLAIMER OF WARRANTY 3

INTRODUCTION 6

CHAPTER 1. THE POWER OF STORYTELLING 8
- My Early Experiences 8
- Why is Storytelling so important? 9

CHAPTER 2. UNDERSTANDING METAPHORS 16
- Simple Metaphors 16
- Extended Metaphors 16
- An Extended Metaphor Example 17
- The Linking to your Message 18

CHAPTER 3. THE SCOPE OF METAPHOR AND STORY 20
- What constitutes a Story or Metaphor? 20
- Anecdotes 20
- Case Studies 20
- Documentaries 21
- Examples 21
- Jokes and Humour 21
- Limericks 22
- Poems 23
- Quotes 23
- Scenarios 24
- Speeches 24
- Studies, Research and Experiments 27
- Success Stories 27
- Videos 28

CHAPTER 4. CREATING YOUR OWN METAPHORS – A SEVEN STEP PROCESS 30
- Step 1 – Get Clarity on your Message 31
- Step 2 - Find something with which your Audience can connect 32
- Step 3 – Make Direct Comparisons to your Message and Metaphor 34
- Step 4 – Create a Short Story from your Metaphor 36
- Step 5 – Connect the Metaphor to the Message 37
- Step 6 – Make a Call to Action 38
- Step 7 - Cement the Learnings 39

CHAPTER 5. THE LANGUAGE OF STORIES 42
- The Importance of using Sensory based Language 43
- Examples of Sensory Descriptors 44
- K.I.S.S! 45
- Boundaries of Language 45

CHAPTER 6. STORYTELLING AND PERSONALITY TYPE 48

CHAPTER 7. STORYTELLING IN BUSINESS AND PUBLIC SPEAKING 52
- The role of Social Media in Storytelling for Business 55
- Conveying Your Message with Metaphors and Analogies 56
- Additional Applications of Stories 57
- Guidelines and Tips for finding Analogies and Metaphors 58
- Guidelines and Tips for using Analogies and Metaphors 60

CHAPTER 8. SOURCING EXAMPLES FOR BUSINESS AND SPEAKER STORIES 62
- Take your People to the Movies 64
- Other Peoples' Stories 66
- Your Stories 66
- Brainstorming and Extraction 67

    Additional ways to Source your Stories 70

CHAPTER 9. LEARNING STYLES – AN INTRODUCTION TO THE 4MAT 72

CHAPTER 10. THE SECRET MAGIC INGREDIENTS 76

    1. Preparing for your Audience 76
    2. Mastering your Delivery 77
    Your Voice 77
    Your Breathing 79
    Use of Pauses and Silence 79
    Use of Suspense and Surprise 80
    Use of Character in Story 80
    Audience Interaction 81
    Use of Questions 81
    Eye Contact 83
    Facial Expressions 84
    Some of us are more naturally expressive than others and the degree to which you use facial expressions in your storytelling is, of course, up to you. If you do feel comfortable however, then your expressions can add another dimension of life to your story. 84
    Deliberate Gestures – The Satir Categories 84
    Movement and Spontaneity 87
    Stage Anchoring 88
    Tense - Past or Present? 88
    Person - First or Third? 89
    I'm Just like You 89
    Little Learning Gems 90
    Use of Reverse Psychology 91
    Planned Spontaneity 91
    Props as Gifts, Giveaways or Product 94
    Stimulus and Response 95
    Step 1 – Know your Goal 98
    Step 2 – Know your Desired Outcome 99
    Step 3 – Know your Audience 99
    Step 4 – Identify the WIIFM (what's in it for me?) for your Listener 100
    Step 5 – Identify the Little Learning Gems 100
    Step 6 – Compile and Structure your Story 101
    Step 7 – Cement the Learnings 105
    Example - Simple Story with Structure 105

CHAPTER 13. POSITIONING YOUR STORY 110

    To Set the Scene 110
    As an Opening Metaphor 110
    As a Pace Changer 111
    As the Body 111
    As a Closing Metaphor 112

CHAPTER 14. HOW TO REMEMBER STORIES 114

    Repetition 114
    Pictures 114
    Using the Clock Numbers 116
    Link'ING' Words 116
    Playback 116
    Story Sketching 116

MY STORY IN A NUTSHELL 117

A SPRINKLING OF MAGIC – YOUR FEEDBACK IS APPRECIATED 118

101 INSPIRING STORIES AND METAPHORS FOR BUSINESS AND LIFE 119

101 INSPIRING QUOTES FOR BUSINESS AND LIFE 120

INTRODUCTION

Stories have captured our minds, hearts and imaginations since before we could talk and they still hold that magic ability to transfer, transmit and transform our message so that it is uniquely understood by every listener.

The aim of this book is to take you on a journey of practicality balanced with imagination and to provide you with a selection of valuable tools, tips, techniques and strategies to further enhance your levels of confidence and expertise in being a master storyteller - whether personally or professionally.

Storytelling today is as important as it ever was, if not more so. In this world of information overload, technology dependence and super speedy shortcuts, it is the stories that we remember. Stories bring to life the messages and lessons that we want to convey. It is through our stories that people will have their 'aha' moments, gain insights into themselves and their values and find ways to contribute to the world that will make the greatest use of their talents and gifts.

'A Sprinkling of Magic' is a special hybrid of a book and a course or guide. I have deliberately sequenced the content so you can follow the steps to creating your own metaphors and stories and, along the way, be able to capture your thoughts and ideas on paper. This is a workbook and is expected to be scribbled on, underlined, highlighted and used time and again, so please don't worry about being precious with it!

This guide is specifically designed to help business leaders, facilitators, speakers, teachers, trainers, writers and communicators to deliver their message in a way that the meaning is understood and assimilated. It's a culmination of my years as a manager and leader in corporate business and as an inspired public speaker and facilitator. I have included everything I have learned along the way, from my love of English at school to my years of learning, using and sharing Neuro Linguistic Programming (NLP), applied social cognitive neuroscience and what has worked (or not) during my years as a people manager on a mission to motivate.

When I talk about stories, I'm not just referring to fairy tales and folklore, fables and parables; it's a far broader scope. I encapsulate how we can share our experiences with others for effect, and how we elaborate on facts and figures to give them meaning and context. People remember stories far more than dry data. I am inspired to help you not just engage your audiences but to captivate them.

You don't have to be eloquent; you don't have to be polished and you don't have to be perfect, you just have to go out and start telling your stories ... preferably with a Sprinkling of Magic!

Read, digest, experiment, practise, share and enjoy the journey.

Chapter One

The Power of Storytelling

Chapter 1. The Power of Storytelling

My Early Experiences

"Are you sitting comfortably? Then I'll begin ..."

These words were spoken every day at 1.45pm as my mother settled me down on her lap to hear a daily storytelling program on BBC Radio called *'Listen with Mother'*. Storytelling was a significant part of my childhood. My Father was a great storyteller and I would cherish our time together at the weekends when he would recount the adventures of Marco Polo, the marvels of the Aurora Borealis and many of the Hans Christian Andersen stories.

As an adult in business, I increasingly understood the power of stories in bringing people with me to work together as a team, understand one another better and accept and embrace difference. It was in sharing my own stories that people came to see the person behind the title, in all her strengths and vulnerabilities, and this led me to my lifelong quest to become a good manager.

In 1996 I was introduced to Neuro Linguistic Programming (NLP) and another layer of sophistication was added to my storytelling repertoire. I learnt how to use a special type of metaphor to help people make the changes they desired in their lives and to find their own solutions to their unique problems.

We are well aware of the particular significance storytelling has in ancient and indigenous cultures. I was born in the United Kingdom and currently live in Australia where, for the indigenous Australians, stories are the essence of who they are, as the story of creation is passed down through the Dreamtime.

Elders around the world continue to educate the younger generations and pass down their values, heritage and traditions through story. In many cultures still today, these laws are not written, yet they have lost none of their gravitas.

Today I use stories and metaphors liberally, yet selectively, in my workshops and speaking engagements. Each and every story I recount is delivered in a different way, according to the audience's needs and of all the positive feedback I receive, it's the stories that seem to resonate most. My aim for you is to reconnect with the power and magic of story, just like you did as a child.

A Sprinkling of Magic

Why is Storytelling so important?

"If history were taught in the form of stories, it would never be forgotten"
Rudyard Kipling

Stories enable us to share truths without the confrontation. We give and are given permission to uncover 'the elephant in the room' - without naming it. We can begin to address challenges, issues, problems and conflicts without coming across as preaching, condescending or having an 'I know better' attitude.

For example, have you ever been on the receiving end of a diatribe, a patronising 'telling off' from the boss, where it's been made very clear that *"things have to change around here"*?

What impact has this had on you? Have you ever come away from a dressing down feeling great? Have you ever been hauled over the coals and given orders to "change your attitude or else", then walked away in gratitude and immediately changed your behaviour?

NO

There's a good reason why stories have been used for centuries to convey laws, values, traditions and, in more modern terms, best practice. It is because they are **a respectful and universally accepted mode of communication**.

I'm not advocating never getting to the point, yet, in my experience, storytelling can be a most effective foundation layer for the subsequent conversations that need to be had. An invitation to reconsider our thinking or behaviour is often best wrapped up in the form of story.

To illustrate my point, I would like to share a story with you that illustrates the importance of storytelling:

There once lived two amazing creatures, one called Truth and the other called Story. Each was beautiful in her own way, but how could they determine which was the most beautiful? They decided that each would walk down the street and whichever creature was befriended the most would be considered the most beautiful.

A coin was tossed and Truth was to go first.

Along the street Truth paraded, sashaying here and there, but rather than gathering friends, doors were closing behind her until she found herself at the end of the street, alone and crying. "I know," she said, "I shall show myself totally naked and the villagers will not be able to resist me." So off came the clothes and Truth returned along the path in all her naked glory.

A Sprinkling of Magic

Far from the welcome she was expecting, not only did people return to their homes, they closed the shutters on their windows and locked their doors. Everyone hated naked Truth.

Truth, naked and cold, had been turned away from every door in the village. Her nakedness frightened the people. When Story found her, Truth was huddled in a corner, shivering and hungry. Taking pity on her, Story gathered her up and took her home.

"Here Truth, take my mantle and go once again into the streets of the village," said Story.

Clothed in the mantle of Story, Truth walked once more down the village street and watched as the doors and shutters opened and the villagers came out into the street smiling and ready to hear what Story had to share.

[This story is based on a Jewish parable attributed to Rabbi Jacob Kranz, an 18th century Eastern European storyteller and teacher who was a also known as the Maggid of Dubbno]

Reading this parable needs no or little explanation (in my opinion). It conveys the message beautifully and paints a vivid picture for the listener.

Stories are unique to the Individual

It is for good reason that I do not provide an interpretation of each of the 101 Inspiring Stories and Metaphors for Business and Life (an e-book available on Amazon). And no, it's not because I am lazy!

As unique individuals with varying histories, experiences, perceptions, beliefs and backgrounds, our interpretation of the story being told is equally unique. You only have to watch 2 politicians going head-to-head after an 'event' or listen to 2 passionate football fans, each defending why and how their side lost, to see that it's all in the interpretation.

If I tell you my version of the moral of the story directly, I am potentially limiting you, the listener from finding alternative meanings, making unique links and forming additional learnings. I may also come across as undermining your intelligence which could break rapport. There is a small caveat here which is linked to the next section and to personality, so be sure to read on to get the whole picture.

We are born Experts in Storylistening

How long have we been listening to stories? Hopefully, for the majority of you, the answer would be 'most of our lives'. We are conditioned from very early on, sometimes from the womb, to listen to stories and be whisked off into new worlds of learning and creation, so much so that, like Pavlov's dogs who ended up salivating at the ring of a bell (because they knew that food was coming), the very mention of the word 'story' brings our awareness to attention - which means we are open to listening.

A Sprinkling of Magic

I am not talking about manipulation or putting groups of people into trance to accept whatever you have to say (which as a qualified hypnotherapist I know isn't possible anyway); I am talking about using a medium for communication that allows the receiver of the message to develop and subsequently therefore 'own' their individual interpretation and lesson.

The Neuroscience of Story

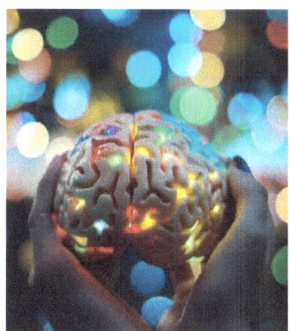

When we listen to dry facts and data, there are very few networks activated in the left hemisphere of the brain (mostly Broca's and Wernicke's), but when we listen to story it becomes a neural, whole brain party!

Different parts of our brain are responsible for different functions e.g. the logical sequence of the story, the literal language and comprehension, the facts, the chronological development and the rationale are functions of certain networks in the brain.

Separate areas of our brain are responsible for painting the pictures, making patterns and connections, seeking meaning and finding the emotion in the story. Combined, they create the memorable story.

We store these memories in different parts of our brain. For example, long term knowledge and facts are stored in the Cerebellum, recent knowledge and facts in the Prefrontal Cortex, experiences of the past in the Hippocampus and certain emotional memories in the Amygdala. The memory of learning a skill resides in the Basal Ganglia.

When we recall a memory, it's a complex process of retrieval and filtering from different parts of the brain and often this memory can be 'enhanced' or 'embellished' as it is recalled. This may not be exactly the biological or scientific explanation, but it is one that you and I can both understand.

To illustrate my point, can you ever remember arguing with a sibling because you have both recalled the same event from the past and are describing it completely differently? In a way you are both right, as each person has a unique interpretation of the event and, having taken 'the long road to recall' from different parts of the brain, it's no wonder.

So, if this happens, just agree to disagree and laugh the next time it occurs!

Stories can bypass the Conscious Mind

When we are in storylistening mode we move into a state of altered consciousness; a light trance so to speak. When were you most read stories to as a child? Probably at bedtime, and why did our guardians read to us at bedtime, usually to get us to go to sleep. The brain forms and deepens connections from all the times we have listened to stories and creates a relationship to the original stimulus e.g. relaxation, escapism, fantasy etc.

Our memory acts like a string of pearls, where experiences are linked together and, like the formation of layers of nacre, are strengthened every time they are repeated. This 'wiring' is particularly strong in the first seven years of life when our brains will make more neural connections than at any other time of our life.

Think back to a time when you read your favourite book – did it become more boring with every reading? No, in fact it was quite the opposite, with excitement building - so much so that if the reader dared to skip a chapter or miss even one word, regardless of how sleepy you were, you catapulted them back to the present moment and corrected them!

When we are in this mild trance state, our subconscious mind is more open to receiving and our conscious mind, together with our (potentially limiting) beliefs, attitudes, opinions and values, takes a 'back seat'. We get out of our own way, so to speak and become more receptive. Don't underestimate this fact when it comes to wanting to help people see a particular situation from a different perspective. No-one will ever do what they don't want to do, however, they will be more open to considering new perspectives when in this receptive mode.

In business, think about when you are bringing a disparate group of people together for a new project or you are embarking on a major change initiative. How useful, effective and important is it to have everyone more open to alignment of the strategy, objectives, values and behaviours that will maximise the success of the project?

Stories Stick

Graphic representation of Synaptic Connections

When we're presented with a story, a metaphor, or any engaging learning that is new, the brain kicks into gear and literally lights up.

Our brain contains around 79 billion neurons, each with around 10,000 synaptic connections - that's about a quadrillion, give or take a few. (Quadrillion = 1,000,000,000,000,000). These synaptic connections fire off and we create new neural pathways when we learn something new.

The first time we learn something new, it's like a human leaping a huge chasm – the first leap is the hardest. Once we repeat the learning (or something very similar to it) it becomes easier each time, as does our ability to recall the information or make use of it. This is why we always encourage people to share or teach what they have just learnt, so that they can cement those learnings in their own neurology.

A Sprinkling of Magic

The more captivating the story, the more our neurology will fire, the deeper our learning is embedded and the more thoroughly the message is understood and the lesson learned. We also increase the chance of learnings being applied and implemented.

When it comes to lighting up our brains, there's a memorable saying that originates from Donald Webb called Hebb's Law:

"What Fires Together, Wires Together"

Stories go Deep

When we listen to a story we are listening on multiple levels, both consciously and subconsciously. As creatures of meaning, our brains start to sort for similarities with the story that is being told and start to form connections. These connections might bring up memories that are stored in distributed areas of our brain and, as mentioned previously, each time they are recalled, they are slightly changed.

Because stories infiltrate at the deep structure or subconscious level, they can make a strong impact on us and inspire us to change behaviour where other methods of imparting information have been less successful. The deeper the lesson is learned, the easier it is to change behaviour or thinking as new neural pathways are formed and shaped.

We connect with Stories

Why do many people love soap operas? It's often because they can relate to the characters and see themselves in the plots and storylines. Soap operas often reflect the real-life trials, tribulations and triumphs of our own lives. This is no different from the stories that we tell and why we find our audience so quickly synthesising with the storyline.

Because we are creatures seeking meaning, as we listen, we start to identify with the characters, the situation or the message. This is a fundamental success criterion for why stories work. Once we've identified with the story, we can then link it back to our unique reality and we may be more open to discussing the meaning in the message and expanding our levels of understanding.

Stories give us permission to be human, to have our quirks and foibles and to relate to the rollercoaster of life. We see ourselves as victim and victor, hero and villain.

Stories let us know that it's okay to be us, warts and all.

---

[2] From 1929 - 1950 the behavioural psychologist Karl Lashley conducted a series of experiments on rats to identify the part of the brain where memories are stored. He trained the rats to find their way through a maze then removed different parts of the cerebral cortex to identify and locate the 'memory trace'. He was unsuccessful as the rats that had parts of their brains cut or removed were still able to find their way through the maze. He concluded that memories are not stored in any single area of the brain; rather they are distributed throughout it.

A Sprinkling of Magic

We all want to be the Hero at some stage

Joseph Campbell in his book 'The Hero with a Thousand Faces' (first published 1949) takes us back to the beginning of time, of stories and tales of mythology that all follow a structured path and have done so for thousands of years, across all cultures.

This path includes a call to adventure and the initial refusal of that call, through fear or a sense of obligation. There then follows the many trials, challenges, adventures and temptations and at some point, following commitment to the journey, a wise guide appears. When you share your story, you are effectively being that wise guide and enabling your audience to embrace and uncover the hero within.

Authors, scriptwriters and film producers have used Campbell's structure called 'The Monomyth' to great success in films such as 'The Wizard of Oz', 'Star Wars', 'Lord of the Rings' and 'Harry Potter'. When we enter their world, we become lost in the story and emerge from the cinema feeling strangely strong and, well, rather heroic!

George Lucas, the Director and Producer of 'Star Wars', worked actively with Campbell in the development of the characters and the plot. He also used ancient temperament theory (personality type) when developing the personalities of his main characters.

Songwriters such as Bob Dylan, Jim Morrison (The Doors) and Jerry Garcia (Grateful Dead) consciously used the heroes' stories and weaved them into their song writing.

Stories transcend Time and Technology

Fads may come and go. Who knows through which medium we will be accessing our information, knowledge and entertainment in 30 years' time? What will still be alive and kicking I imagine, will be the power of the story, told face to face, in families and communities, in offices and on stages everywhere.

With the advent and emergence of artificial intelligence, people can become even more immersed and engaged in stories, helping to shape the storylines, and advertisers are using this to huge advantage as they tease their fans; for example before the launch of a new book or movie. See also the section on stories for business and in Chapter 7.

In Summary

Stories are as old as the human race and are hard wired into our neurology as an engaging, respectful and effective way to communicate our message and the lessons of life. As you read through the book, your scope of what constitutes a 'story' may expand.

If, at this stage, you are more comfortable listening to stories than telling them, follow the progress through each of the chapters to build skills, structure and style.

Chapter Two

Understanding Metaphors

CHAPTER 2. UNDERSTANDING METAPHORS

While I was blessed to have a passionate English teacher at school, I don't want to become hung up (oops – that's a metaphor) on definitions of metaphor in the strictest sense. What I share with you in this book is my perception and interpretation of metaphor.

The word metaphor has its origin in Latin and Greek, with *'metaphora'* meaning *'to carry over* or *transfer'*. Our aim in using metaphors is to **transfer the meaning to a different concept where the message can be uniquely and universally understood.** We refer to two types of metaphors in this guide:

Simple Metaphors involve using language that isn't literal to illustrate or describe a situation in a way that the listener can depict it and interpret it.

Examples of simple metaphors:

- *The decision was difficult to swallow.* (We can't swallow decisions)
- *She was a great catch.* (Maybe if she was fired directly from a cannon and hopefully weighed under 40kg/90lb)
- *The prosecution grilled the witness.* (Ouch!)

Each of these simple examples brings an added dimension to the sentence. If instead we heard "the decision was difficult to accept", "she was very attractive" or "the prosecution asked challenging questions", it's a little more dry and boring.

A common definition of a metaphor is *'A comparison that shows how two things that are not alike in most ways are similar in another important way'* (Wikipedia). If you use the words 'like' or 'as' then, strictly speaking, this is a simile – however a simile is also a type of metaphor.

Extended Metaphors are what we will concentrate on in this guide. Extended metaphors or allegory are short stories or comparisons that we use to describe situations in which everyone can elicit their own interpretation or meaning.

Often used metaphors that you may be familiar with include:

Love is a Battlefield – maybe if you've been hurt in love, you might say that you fought, lost and are now scarred, and you may not have physically done any of these things. Military analogies are often used as metaphors for survival and winning through in the end, for leadership or for suffering.

Business is a Game of Chess – you need an overall game plan yet have to be flexible. You need to think strategically, anticipating your competitor's moves and be ready to make an unpredictable move or take a risk. You need to understand the value of the role of every piece on the board, the 'pieces' being other stakeholders.

An Extended Metaphor Example

For the grammarians among us, this is strictly considered an analogy.

The Ladder of Learning

A metaphor that many trainers and facilitators are familiar with is the comparison of learning to drive with learning new skills and adopting new ways of operating. It's called 'The Ladder of Learning'. This story is based on learning to drive a manual car and can be adapted for automatic transmission.

Stage 1 – Unconscious Incompetence

Can you remember being in the car as a kid and thinking: *"This driving malarkey is a cinch. All you have to do is put your feet on some pedals, move a stick and turn a wheel – easy peasy!"*

This is the **'we don't know what we don't know'** stage, otherwise known as being unconsciously incompetent or blissfully ignorant!

Stage 2 – Conscious Incompetence

The time comes when we reach that magical age – whoo hoo – time to get my driving license! So, we get our learner's permit then jump in a car with some poor victim, often a parent. We turn the key and what happens next? We kangaroo hop down the road and stall at every available and inappropriate moment!

We are officially consciously incompetent - i.e. **we now know what we don't know**.

Stage 3 – Conscious Competence

A few dozen or hundred lessons later, we pass our driving test and have the piece of paper to prove it. This is where we really start to learn to drive.

Our first time in the car alone, we turn on the engine, look in the mirror in an overly exaggerated manner, signal and then manoeuvre. We engage the clutch, change gear then place our hands back on the wheel in a '10 to 2 o'clock' position. We are aware of our every movement and that of every other car on the road.

We now know what we know and can be considered consciously competent.

Stage 4 – Unconscious Competence

After many years of driving we jump in the car, turn on the engine, set off, turn on the radio, make phone calls (hands free of course), chat with our passengers, eat and drink, then arrive at our destination - sometimes not even remembering how we got there.

The process is now embedded in our subconscious mind, so much so that it's become automatic to us. **We now no longer know what we know**, so can be considered officially unconsciously competent.

Stage 5 – Re-conscious Competence

Stage 5 is my own creation and addition from experience. So, you're a confident and unconsciously competent driver, then you travel overseas and rent a car where the steering wheel is not only on the other side but so is all of the traffic!

All of a sudden you start to make silly mistakes like leaving the handbrake on and indicating in the wrong direction. You stall - which you haven't done for years - and you cut people off, even drive down a one-way street the wrong way. What's happening?

Your brain is taking all the differences into account and bringing you back to a level which will probably keep you safe. You have officially and temporarily been relegated to the world of the consciously (in)competent!

You can also drop back to conscious competence after an accident, until you have regained your confidence.

The Linking to your Message

So, imagine you've told your story about driving; now you need to make the parallel and link driving with whatever your key message is. I prefer to make the link by asking questions rather than pointing out the parallels. I would usually start by simply asking:

- So how is X (X being the new skills) like learning to drive?
- What examples can you give me of being unconsciously competent? (then go through each stage)
- What might help us to transition each stage more effectively and speedily?
- What else do we need to be aware of?
- What will we do if we find ourselves dropping back a stage?
- What will it take in terms of attitude and commitment to reach Stage 4?
- How will we know that we've achieved unconscious competence?

We're no longer talking about driving – we've elegantly transitioned, thanks to the magic of metaphor, to the real situation at hand.

Chapter Three

The Scope of Metaphor and Story

CHAPTER 3. THE SCOPE OF METAPHOR AND STORY

What constitutes a Story or Metaphor?

This is an important distinction to make, as we often think of a story in terms of our childhood connections. We don't need to start our story with *"Once Upon a Time"*, that is, unless you want to alienate most of the cynics and sceptics in your adult audience.

We are using the words 'story' and 'metaphor' as a catchall for conveying information and messages to our audience in a captivating and engaging manner. There are many ways to do this and below are a few examples.

Anecdotes

Anecdotes are recollections of real events that happened, in effect real life stories. They can be about yourself and people you know or about people, places and things that happened in history. Where we might use some poetic license with our own stories, anecdotes are usually shared 'as is'.

If you're going to share an anecdote about someone you don't know, make sure it's accurate and not an urban myth. If you receive a great 'true' story and want to use it to effect, check its validity first or you could lose your audience. There are websites such as Hoax Slayer and Snopes that can help with validation.

A well-known example of an anecdote that is an urban myth is the story that the father of Alexander Fleming, who discovered penicillin and saved a young Winston Churchill from drowning. The story is a great metaphor for the law of reciprocity; however, we could lose credibility if we were to relay it as true.

Case Studies

A case study is also a story. Like an anecdote, it should also be true (a made-up case study becomes a scenario). Case studies are used in business to provide validity and credibility as to the performance of the people or product involved. They can also be invaluable in helping people avoid certain pitfalls and mistakes.

For example, many years ago, I was Director of Customer Service for an Internet Service Provider and found myself in the unenviable position of making a large number of people redundant. The approach we took, the systems we used and the attitude we adopted, all led to the most favourable outcome for everyone that we could have wished for.

When I break down each of these elements and document them, I have a case study of 'How to let People go with Professionalism and Dignity' and can use it with clients facing similar challenges.

The core of the case study should include:

- The outline
- Challenges faced or problems presented
- Approaches considered
- Results achieved
- Reasons for results and key lessons learned

Where appropriate all relevant statistics should be provided.

Documentaries

Making a documentary of your business history for example is a highly effective way for new employees to understand your roots and culture and for existing employees to remain engaged. Even better – have your staff make the documentary. Documentaries are also more engaging for practical, rational viewers and listeners whilst also engaging those with creative preferences.

Generations X and Y have grown up with reality TV and so are familiar with documentary style storytelling.

Examples

Examples are the missing piece of the jigsaw when it comes to sharing information or teaching something new. They are mini stories with meanings and help cement learning by providing a clear connection and context for the listener. By providing examples, you are also validating your credibility.

If you are going to make bold statements, be prepared to back them up with examples as this will address the cynics and sceptics in your audience. If you want audience interaction, then ask <u>them</u> for some examples to back up your point.

Marketing guru, author and thought leader Seth Godin is a master storyteller, peppering his presentations with relevant examples and stories. When I watch him, I can see that he is following a simple process:

1. What's the point I want to make?
2. Outline with a story or example
3. Make the point

Jokes and Humour

A joke can be, but is not necessarily, a funny story. I have been lucky enough to see Billy Connolly live and he is a true master storyteller. I came away feeling like I had done 1000 sit ups, I was so sore, yet I could not recollect any specific stories until a few days later (which he told us would happen).

A Sprinkling of Magic

I wouldn't necessarily advocate using jokes in your storytelling unless you are either naturally funny or prepared to work hard at it. What I would encourage though is the use of humour. Humour is a strong bridge builder and can be used to great effect as an ice breaker, creating rapport with your audience and putting them at ease.

When I have a speaking engagement, I try to find something from the news that is topical and funny to share and it makes for an effective opening. Let me share with you something that I found in the 'London Evening News' and shared with my group. The title of our workshop was 'Communicating for Effect' and I think these London Underground Train Drivers achieved this very well!

> *"Please note that the beeping noise coming from the doors means that the doors are about to close. It does not mean throw yourself or your bags into the doors.*
>
> *Your delay this evening is caused by the Line Controller suffering from E & B Syndrome, this means not knowing his elbow from his backside. I'll let you know any further information as soon as I'm given some, which probably won't be anytime soon.*
>
> *Do you want the good news first or the bad news? The good news is that last Friday was my birthday and I hit the town and had a great time, what I remember of it anyway. The bad news is that there is a points failure somewhere between Stratford and East Ham, which means we probably won't reach our destination."*

Limericks

Limericks are funny five-line ditties that have a specific rhyming pattern. Some of you will be more familiar with limericks than others. Lines 1, 2, and 5 have seven to ten syllables and rhyme with one another. Lines 3 and 4 have five to seven syllables and also rhyme with each other.

Most limericks around aren't printable for general publication! It's easier to give you examples, so here's one I remember as a child, written by Edward Lear who was a master of limerick.

A wonderful bird is the pelican
His bill can hold more than his belican
He can take in his beak
Food enough for a week
But I'm damned if I see how the helican!

A Sprinkling of Magic

I also found this business-related limerick on 'Business Pundit'

If increasing sales is your need
What your customers say, you should heed
Listen to their suggestions
Or face insurrections
Which decreases your sales with great speed!

Imagine how much more fun problem solving in business could be if we challenged all staff to come up with a great limerick? There is power in lateral thinking.

Poems

How many of you have considered sharing a poem as an inspirational message? No? Open your mind! There are so many poems out there that are metaphors for courage, resilience, adapting to change, taking responsibility, leadership etc.

Remembering that we all have differing learning preferences, it could be that a poem is the one way of communicating 'that specific message' to that 'inflexible listener' and make all the difference. I have included some of my favourite inspirational poems in 101 Inspiring Stories and Metaphors for Business and Life which is in electronic form (see back of book).

Similar to the limerick, you might want to set a challenge to your people to write a company poem or a poem that reflects the people or organisational culture.

Quotes

A quotation is like a mini power-packed story. It can be the magic ingredient in the recipe that brings out all the flavours of the metaphorical dish. If you want to credibly support your theory, then to do so with a powerful quote sets the scene perfectly.

For example, if I'm working with business leaders and I want them to move from being task-focused to looking at the bigger picture, or WHY they are in business - then this quote below from French writer and aviator Antoine de Saint-Exupery is what I might use to open the discussion:

"If you want to build a ship, don't drum up people together to collect wood and don't assign them tasks and work, but rather teach them to long for the sea."

I may then throw it open for comment and interpretation to set the context.

To add extra credibility, learn a little about the author of the quote, always attribute the author (unless it's anonymous or unknown) and make sure that you have the correct author. I have seen some great philosopher's quotes being falsely attributed to politicians and celebrities – ouch!

Scenarios

Scenarios can be as compelling as any story. In fact, scenarios are an excellent way to involve your audience and have them provide the solutions by creating the ending to the story. Scenarios can be either fictional or real depending on your focus on the process or the content.

An example of a process based fictional problem-solving scenario that is used in teambuilding is that of the 'Life Raft Survivor' game where the team is given a scenario of being capsized at sea, in the lifeboat and in possession of 15 items that they have to agree the order of importance and why.

It's not so much about getting the list right but observing the team members and how they listen to each other, make decisions, compromise and negotiate.

A simple example of a real-life content-based scenario might be the 'Boss for a Day' scenario. Each team member will be given the opportunity to run the company or department for a day and make decisions, solve problems and handle crises with all the authority of the boss. You can then give each individual a different scenario, preferably concrete examples of challenges that have happened in the past, and they have to solve the problem with their 'boss hat' on.

Not only does the team member experience challenge from 'the other side of the desk', we also get to observe their skills in leadership, ingenuity, decision making and more.

Speeches

If you have a message to deliver and someone has gone before you and found the most articulate, inspiring and motivational way to impart it; why not take a leaf from their metaphorical book and use it to add that extra sprinkling of magic?

A well-crafted speech is a fine balance of reality and metaphor; it uses language that appeals to all the senses and learning styles. It creates a story that sets the scene then follows with a subtle balance of challenge and solution, ending on a call to action - whether physical, emotional or mental - that can effect change.

Reading extracts from the speeches of great orators can provide you with lightbulb moments for your story - without the need to plagiarise. Though this guide isn't about speeches per se, it would be remiss of me not to include them as they have moved masses to action (both at war and in peace) and have an eternal ripple effect.

Take some quality time to read the extracts from the following three speeches that I have found to have used metaphors and analogy so eloquently and powerfully.

A Sprinkling of Magic

Kevin Rudd

I have included the former Prime Minister of Australia, Kevin Rudd's apology speech to the Stolen Generations of Indigenous Australians on 12th February 2008, not only because it is an important element of the history of my country of residence and citizenship, but also to show you that the use of metaphor in short speeches can be highly effective.

From the extract, see how Rudd has used the simple book metaphor to great effect.

"The time has now come for the nation to turn a new page in Australia's history by righting the wrongs of the past and so moving forward with confidence to the future.

For the future we take heart; resolving that this new page in the history of our great continent can now be written.

A future where all Australians, whatever their origins, are truly equal partners, with equal opportunities and with an equal stake in shaping the next chapter in the history of this great country, Australia."

Dr. Martin Luther King Jr.

Martin Luther King Jr's *"I Have a Dream"* speech is, in my opinion, one of the most inspiring of all time. More than 200,000 civil rights supporters of all ethnicities and colour thronged to the steps of the Lincoln Memorial on a sweltering August day in 1963, no social media to share the news, just word of mouth and a groundswell of hope and change.

It was hard to pick just a few excerpts as King was an absolute master of metaphor. You can read the full transcript of his speech in 101 Inspiring Stories and Metaphors for Business and Life and can see how he is appealing to every sense, every creed and every opinion.

Public domain photo from *"I have a Dream"* speech.

His speech is packed to bursting with the values of freedom and justice and if you are sharing stories around values, hope and belief, or a visualisation of the future, then you will be spoilt for choice finding magic in this speech to sprinkle on your message.

Here's a taste:

"But we refuse to believe that the bank of justice is bankrupt. We refuse to believe that there are insufficient funds in the great vaults of opportunity of this nation.

And so, we've come to cash this check, a check that will give us upon demand the riches of freedom and the security of justice.

I have a dream that one day on the red hills of Georgia, the sons of former slaves and the sons of former slave owners will be able to sit down together at the table of brotherhood.

I have a dream that one day even the state of Mississippi, a state sweltering with the heat of injustice, sweltering with the heat of oppression, will be transformed into an oasis of freedom and justice."

Nelson Mandela

Mandela's Inaugural Address Speech is a powerful example of humanity, reconciliation and forgiveness. As someone who was once involved in terrorist activity, he spoke to every individual who wanted retribution and with his words held out an olive branch of peace, offering the country a better chance of healing.

If you are working or dealing with people in conflict, then this speech makes for an empowering case study and discussion.

In these few extracts Mandela uses powerful metaphors that appeal to the different senses and helps create a swell of motion and action.

"The time for the healing of the wounds has come. The moment to bridge the chasms that divide us has come. The time to build is upon us.

We have triumphed in the effort to implant hope in the breasts of the millions of our people.

A rainbow nation at peace with itself and the world.

Let each know that for each the body, the mind and the soul have been freed to fulfil themselves."

I have also included in 101 Inspiring Stories and Metaphors for Business and Life, Shakespeare's *St Crispin's Day' Speech* from the play Henry V, as it is an excellent example of inspiring leadership and motivation. This is the dramatised speech Henry V gave to his heavily outnumbered troops before going into the Battle of Agincourt.

I would also encourage you to research other famous speeches and here are a few more of my favourites:

- Emmeline Pankhurst's *'Freedom or Death'* speech, 13 November, 1913
- Jawaharlal Nehru's *'Independence'* speech, 14 August, 1947
- Oprah Winfrey's 'Truth' speech, 8 January, 2018
- John F Kennedy's *'Man on the Moon'* address, 25 May, 1961
- Barack Obama's *'This is your Victory',* 4 November, 2008

A Sprinkling of Magic

Studies, Research and Experiments

There are some fascinating experiments that have been carried out that can add credibility to and validate your story or theory that you can weave in for effect. It may take a bit of research, but it is well worth the effort. Make sure though that your information is correct and not an urban myth. For example, there is a well-known experiment about Harvard (or sometimes Yale or Stanford) graduates and writing down goals, but none of these universities are aware of its existence. I use a number of studies/experiments in my work. Here are a few for you to consider:

- Gallup's study over 25 years of 1 million employees and 80,000 managers
- Martin Seligman's work with Metropolitan Life Insurance (Optimism)
- Rosenthal and Jacobson's Pygmalion in the Classroom experiment
- The Notre Dame Happy Nun Study – Happiness and longevity

When you reveal validated statistical information in your story, you are directly appealing to the naysayers, sceptics and cynics or those people for whom a rational and logical explanation is essential to adopt a new course of thinking. This information also adds weight and objectivity to your own belief or theory. Make sure you can cite and honour the creators of the experiment/research if asked and that dates etc. are correct.

Sharing data and research doesn't have to be boring. It's all about how you deliver it. More about this in the Secret Magic Ingredients in Chapter 10.

Success Stories

Particularly in business, success stories are worth gold. Well-crafted stories about challenges that were overcome, ideas that made a million, valuable lessons learned from failure, lessons in persistence, accidental inventions etc., are highly effective ways to communicate what you stand for, your culture, your brand and your 'stickiness factor' i.e. why people should want to buy from you, partner with you, work for you, stay with you and grow with you.

When you disseminate your stories and they then permeate throughout all your stakeholder relationships, chances are that you can turn your stories into legends.

Here are a few examples of some of my favourite business success stories:

- Apple's comeback with Steve Jobs
- How Richard Branson started Virgin Airlines
- The story of the Armani suit with Nordstrom
- Johnny the Bagger and Barbara Glanz
- The 3M 'Post It Note' discovery

- The story of Zappo's success with CEO Tony Hsieh (now passed)
- Jim's New York Coffee Stall (in *'Speed of Trust'* by Stephen M R Covey)
- The story of Viagra and its interesting side effect!

Whenever you want to challenge people to rise to the occasion or motivate them to bounce back, finding a success story that is similar to what they are currently experiencing, is the perfect medium and metaphor for action.

Videos

Video is a powerful form of storytelling. It's highly visual, instant, cost-effective, endearing, simple and has already been responsible for the 'rags to riches' stories of countless people and businesses.

In Summary

Our aim is to communicate for effect and leave our audience having given them an experience of which they really felt a part. There are so many ways to deliver your information and add credibility and meaning to your message and in a way that enhances and optimises the learning experience for your audience. Start thinking about your own success stories, tales of challenge, case studies and scenarios to build a rich story database of experience.

Notes, Ideas and Thoughts so far

Chapter Four

Creating your own Metaphors
A Seven Step Process

CHAPTER 4. CREATING YOUR OWN METAPHORS – A SEVEN STEP PROCESS

In this section I share examples of how speakers and storytellers have developed their own metaphors. Please respect their unique and exclusive ownership of these and contact them directly if you would like to know more. Thank you.

So what we are looking to do is to find something our audience can connect with and find the parallels and comparisons. Once we have found a metaphor we think will work, we can try it out. The test of success is whether people continue to speak in the language of the metaphor when referring to their situations.

I once attended a conference where the speaker, Ron Jungalwalla, Managing Director of Quest Group Australia, used the metaphor of a set of golf clubs to discuss styles of leadership, and to great effect. He elaborated his metaphor into a story and asked us to consider the consequences of playing a full round of golf with our favourite club. How long do you think it would take to complete 18 holes with a putter or a driver?

Ron then connected this with leadership styles and recounted examples of leaders who lead solely with their favourite style. Put two and two together and what's the meaning in the message?

Can you see how the golf club analogy makes sense of situational leadership (adapting your leadership style to suit the situation and people)? As a leader, the next time I went to address a particular issue, had I heard Ron speak, I would probably say to myself:

"Now Clare, what leadership style would be most appropriate for this situation and these people? Ah yes, I think I'll take my 9 iron!"

N.B. You must make sure that the metaphor you choose resonates with your audience or you will lose them quickly.

Here's another example. Dr Wayne Dyer (now passed), self-help advocate, author and speaker, tells the story of a man who dropped his keys in the house then went outside to look for them under the streetlight. A friendly neighbour passes by and offers his help, which is graciously accepted. *"Where did you lose the keys?"* enquires the neighbour after a good and fruitless search. *"Oh, in the kitchen,"* replied the man, *"But it's easier to look for them out here."*

Dyer continues by questioning why we so often look for the answers to our troubles outside of ourselves when we instinctively know that the answer lies within. With the keys analogy, it's so clear and even silly, yet when we are questioned directly about our own strategies, it can be confronting or take a while for the penny to drop (pardon the metaphor).

So how do we create our own unique metaphors? Let's get started with a clear seven step process.

Step 1 – Get Clarity on your Message

What is your outcome? For what purpose do you want to use a metaphor? What is the message you want to convey and why is it important? Once you are clear on these points then your brain can start sorting for stories that will help reinforce your message, but **you must be clear on the message first.**

In Step 2 I will take you through a metaphor I created when I was looking for an example of high performing teams and individuality. I wanted an analogy of teamwork where individuality was respected and embraced, yet the need to work together to a common goal was even more important. I also wanted the message to resonate with celebrating and optimising individual strengths, gifts and talents. I wanted the metaphor to illustrate that the whole is greater than the sum of the parts.

When we're clear on the message we can then develop the metaphor.

What is your Message?

Step 2 - Find something with which your Audience can connect

If you are talking to a group of highly spiritual massage therapists then golf stories, I suspect, might not be the most appropriate route! Aim to keep your comparison in line with your audience's interests (or at least the majority of them) or use an analogy that can be recognised by all and won't cause a break in rapport, loss of interest or confusion.

Sadly, too many times I have either been in the audience or been on the speaker's list when someone comes out on stage and recounts endless stories about subjects that really aren't in synch with the audience (sports storytellers being the greatest culprits).

One way to get the brain stimulated to find a relevant metaphor is to ask yourself *"X is/are"….*or *"X is like….."* (X being the subject you want to make a comparison with). Keep going until you can't think of any more then push at least twice because it's often through that blank spot that you get your best ideas.

Aim to find a balance of creativity and practicality. For example, I can think of nature-based analogies for teams such as a flock of geese, a colony of ants or a herd of elephants, however using the whooping crane (birds) of Australia as an example might be a little too obscure (despite them being great team workers!).

A Symphony Orchestra – an Effective Metaphor for High Performing Teams

The perfect metaphor I found for my high performing teams was that of a symphony orchestra. I asked myself *"High performing teams are like … ?"* then came up with many analogies from sport; however they weren't appropriate for my audience. Eventually the words 'harmonious' and 'in tune with one another' popped into my head - and so did the orchestra!

Keep asking yourself, *"How else is this like X? How else, how else?"* or *"What else does X do that reinforces my message?"* If you try this with a few examples, you'll know you've found 'the one' when you can apply it as broadly as possible to the message you want to deliver.

A Sprinkling of Magic

Chunking - in addition to using comparisons (which is an example of chunking sideways), you can play the 'chunking' game. This is where you ask yourself, *"of what is X a part or example?"* (chunking up) or *"what is a part of X?"* (chunking down). The easiest way I can explain this is to use an example of a car:

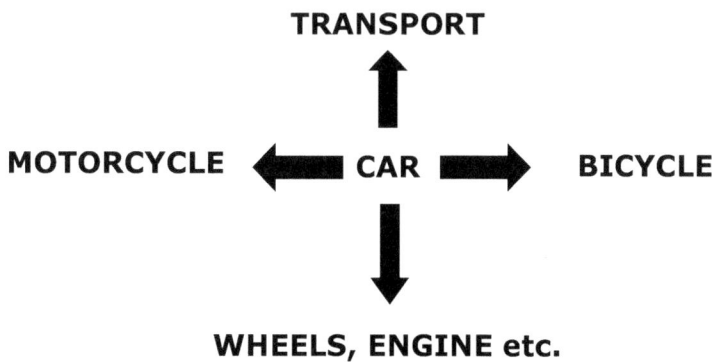

What Themes might your Audience connect with?

Expand the Analogies - keeping with my orchestra, I brainstormed everything about a world class symphony orchestra that was in alignment with my message and found an abundance of extra valuable comparisons. For example, the leader of a world class orchestra selects the most talented musicians AND they must also be able to interact with and respect the other musicians; they also doesn't tolerate divas when they play up. Can you imagine an orchestra filled with 'wannabe' soloists? It would sound terrible, and the team would soon fall apart. The orchestra is clear on its musical masterpiece and works together to create a unique, harmonious sound.

There are about 90 instruments in a symphony orchestra and every musician knows what contribution they and their instrument make to the collective experience. The piece of music has probably been played by hundreds of orchestras, but what makes this one uniquely different?

A world class orchestra has a conductor who can lead with authority yet totally tune in to every member individually. They have a global perspective and trust the musicians to do their job well, every time.

A Sprinkling of Magic

The conductor is supported by the first violinist who plays a fundamental role in communicating with other members. There are many more analogies and examples, but these should provide you with some food for thought.

What are some possible Analogies for your chosen Message?

Step 3 – Make Direct Comparisons to your Message and Metaphor

World Class Symphony Orchestra	**High Performing Team**
Selects the most talented musicians that can also interact with other musicians. Doesn't tolerate divas when they play up	Selects for talent yet can still be a team player Does not tolerate 'diva like' behaviour – expectations, values, standards and boundaries are clear
Is clear on its musical masterpiece and works together to create a unique sound	Has a clear team purpose and goal, knows that what it needs to create is unique and will surpass that of other teams
The piece of music has probably been played by hundreds of orchestras but what makes this one different?	Their product may be hard to differentiate, but what is it about the way they work together that differentiates them to be able to provide world class service?
There are about 90 instruments in a symphony orchestra and everyone knows what contribution they and their instruments make to the experience	There may be a multitude of roles in a team, yet every role is crucial to the whole team performance and every member knows the impact that their contribution makes

A Sprinkling of Magic

World Class Symphony Orchestra	High Performing Team
Each musician specialises in one instrument (maybe two) and is given the opportunity to play their best in every performance	Every team member has a particular strength in one or two areas and, when given the opportunity to shine, will contribute greatly to the whole
Has a conductor who can lead with authority yet totally tunes in to every member individually	Has an emotionally intelligent leader who is able to respect the 'I' in team and manages according to the individual's motivations and drivers
The conductor maintains a global perspective (sees the whole score) and trusts the musicians to perform to their best	An effective leader maintains a strategic perspective and uses trust and confidence to empower managers to manage and trusts that their people will perform
The conductor is supported by the first violinist who plays a fundamental role in communicating with other players	The leader is supported by a 2IC (second in charge) who acts as the catalyst for communication, bridging gaps and making sure information and knowledge is shared

What are some Comparisons you can make for your chosen Metaphor?

Analogy or Example	My Message

Analogy or Example	My Message

Step 4 – Create a Short Story from your Metaphor

I start by asking any of the team members I'm working with if they have ever seen an orchestra or large band play live. It's a good way to set the scene and gauge the level of existing awareness. I may ask a few questions about their experience, favourite bands, musical taste etc. as part of building rapport.

I then continue by sharing a story about the first time I saw the London Symphony Orchestra play at the Royal Albert Hall in London. I limit the amount of information about the actual musical performance but elaborate on my observations of the orchestra as a high performing team.

You can use some poetic license – it may have been a different venue, you may have seen a different orchestra – that's okay – just make sure you are congruent and keep your story believable.

A Sprinkling of Magic

If you can link your metaphor to an experience of your own then great; if not, make one up or create a fictional story. You can still put yourself in the story. For example, I usually put myself and a colleague in the 'Gingernuts at the Airport' story which is a metaphor for the consequences of jumping to conclusions and making assumptions.

If people have heard the story before, they'll forgive you.

I will then link Step 4 to Step 5 by sharing a key part of the message conversationally. For example, *"I've always been curious as to what makes a good orchestra great. How come they don't all start and stop at different times and how can they perform as such a close-knit professional team when they all have different roles to play?"*

Sketch out your short Story

Step 5 – Connect the Metaphor to the Message

This is imperative otherwise your metaphor remains just a story and it may be a story without a message or a meaning. It can also be confusing for people with a natural preference for logic and analysis if the connection is weak.

With the orchestra metaphor, I tend to run an exercise and rather than deliver the connections, I invite the audience to make them by asking a few questions such as:

- So what do you think makes a great orchestra world class?
- What would happen if one of the musicians wanted to stand out from the others and how do you think the orchestra would deal with that?
- What would happen, for example, if the percussionist was feeling left out because they only had a small role and gave up before the climactic cymbal clash?
- What's the role of the conductor and what makes a world class conductor?

A Sprinkling of Magic

Can you see how the messages are coming together? Your audience will be making the connections and comparisons and bringing their own experience into the story. At this stage they will be transferring (remember the origin of the word metaphor) their learnings to their particular situation, and this is when we can invite dialogue about their learnings.

Examples of Connecting Questions

Step 6 – Make a Call to Action

This is where we make the direct comparison and encourage the conversation. In this example I would ask, *"As we are today, if we were an orchestra, what sort of orchestra might we be?"*

I would work with the answers then ask, *"What would it take for us to become the <Company or team name> equivalent of a world class orchestra? What will it take for us to become a world class team?"*

Call to Action Questions

Step 7 - Cement the Learnings

You may want to give a gift connected with your metaphor (I cover this in more detail in the section on Use of Props in Chapter 11) or play a video that reinforces your message or create an activity.

To add a Sprinkling of Magic for my example, I might play some classical music in the background at the end of the session or during reflections (if this is a workshop) or show a clip of a highly animated conductor playing a well-known piece of music.

To add to the experience and to bring some teambuilding and humour, I give each team member a musical instrument and ask them to compose a piece of music and play it within 20 minutes, often with hilarious results. I have had great success tasking teams to create their own instruments and give them one week to come up with a team jingle. It's about getting creative and making it memorable.

Ways to Cement the Learnings

In Summary

By using analogies and metaphors, I have invested time and energy to build a relationship, gain permission, set the scene and allow a discussion to take place that might have, had it been dealt with directly, resulted in a less productive or even defensive exchange of views.

Where the difficult and challenging conversations still need to be had, metaphors and stories can pave the way and lay the foundations for respectful dialogue. You still though, pardon the metaphoric pun, need to address the elephant in the room regardless of approach.

Now that you have a clear example of your metaphor, you will start to see them popping up everywhere, so I recommend you keep notes and capture them.

Putting it all together

Now see how you can start to structure the metaphor bringing all 7 steps together.

First Draft Metaphor

Chapter Five

The Language of Stories

A Sprinkling of Magic

CHAPTER 5. THE LANGUAGE OF STORIES

Read the following two descriptions out loud and work out what's different about them.

Story 1

> *When I woke up on this morning, I knew it was going to be a special day because it was the 5th of September, the day I was getting married. I felt excited, jumped out of bed and thought about getting ready.*

Story 2

> *As my brain started to crank into gear, I began to stir slowly. Outside the lorikeets were yapping away in competition with the cackling kookaburras. The newly blossomed jasmine plants were bidding me good day with their wafting perfume floating into the bedroom. As I opened the curtains to drink in their scent, the blue sky greeted me like a Picasso on show.*
>
> *The date was the 5th of September and as I became more conscious and awake, it suddenly dawned on me – this was the day I had waited 47 years for, this was my wedding day. My heart felt like the bass beat at a rave – thumping so loud I could hear it! I savoured every second because I was so excited, and I knew time would fly by and I wanted to be in charge of the clock on this auspicious day. I contemplated getting ready.*

Apart from Story 2 being obviously longer, what else is different?

Yes, it's more descriptive than the first story, but how is it more descriptive?

- lorikeets were yapping
- cackling kookaburras
- jasmine plants were bidding me good day with their wafting perfume
- drink in their scent
- savoured every second
- blue sky greeted me like a Picasso on show
- heart felt like the bass beat at a rave

How many of you could hear the birds, smell the jasmine, see the sky and sense my heartbeat and excitement? All of the expressions in story 2 are using sensory language to communicate with you and bring you with me on my storytelling journey. I have exaggerated it for effect and, in reality, would probably use about half of the expressions.

The Importance of using Sensory-based Language

Using sensory-based language to communicate is an essential element of storytelling because we take in information first through our senses.

Our brains process images 60,000 times faster than words and our visual cortex is the largest of all our sensory cortices, so painting a visual picture (if we do not have visual impairment) is guaranteed to make our stories stick. We find it easy to create images and at a subconscious level are connecting with the **visual language** in the story, seeing the birds and the sky and the person in bed.

For some, what is uppermost might be the link to the **olfactory sensations** (smell). The smell of the jasmine wafting through the window may have taken them off to a time when that was true for them, or they may be able to instantly re-create the smell of jasmine in their minds.

Here's a little extra golden nugget for you – of all the senses, smell bypasses the traditional neural pathways of the other senses and can be recalled faster and more vividly than all the other senses. Have you ever smelt the perfume or aftershave of an 'ex' and been instantly catapulted back in time? I rest my case!

Those with a preference for taking in information in an **auditory** sense may have resonated with the sound of the birds and the thumping heartbeat.

The emotions that the story brought up would have been picked up instantly by those with a preference for taking in information **kinaesthetically** (by feeling), so in addition to reading about the excitement and a heart that 'felt like the bass beat', they may have been catapulted back to a similar experience. They may even have noticed an increase in heart rate as they read about the 'thumping so loud' (combining kinaesthetic and visual).

And last but not least – if taste is important to you (maybe you are a budding Master Chef or Wine Taster) then those neurons might have fired up when reading about 'savouring every second' because of your **gustatory** preference.

When we consciously use sensory language to create our stories, we not only bring them to life, we make them all-inclusive. This is where we step from the literal world into the inferential world and our sense of imagery, imagination and emotion is fired up and fully engaged.

A Sprinkling of Magic

Examples of Sensory Descriptors

Here are some more examples of sensory words that you can consciously include in your stories to give them that extra sprinkling of magic!

Visual	Auditory	Kinaesthetic	Olfactory	Gustatory
Appear	Attune	Adhere	Aroma	Aftertaste
Black & White	Bellow	Bump	Bouquet	Bitter
Blinding	Cackle	Clutch	Essence	Bittersweet
Bright	Crash	Comfortable	Fresh	Burnt
Crystal Clear	Harmonise	Cool	Fragrant	Delicious
Dark	Hear	Cosset	Hint of	Devour
Dull	Laugh	Feels like/right	Incense	Digest
Envision	Listen	Firm	Musty	Dine out on
Flash	Loud	Gentle	Nose (for things)	Drink in
Foggy	Muffle	Grasp	Nose (gets up my)	Eat
Focus	Music	Grip	Odour	Flavour
Glance	Noise	Gut feel	Perfume	Hungry
Glare	Orchestrate	Heart	Pungent	Nibble on
Glimpse	Purr	Kick	Putrid	Savour
Glisten	Resonate	Nudge	Rat (smell a)	Season(ed)
Illuminate	Ring	Pierce	Rancid	Snack
Insight	Shout	Scrape	Reek	Sour
Mind's eye	Silence	Shake	Scent	Spice
Murky	Speak	Sharp	Smell	Stale
Overlook	Tinkle	Soft	Smokey	Swallow
Picture	Tone	Stick	Sneeze at	Sweet
Reveal	Trickle	Stomach	Sniff at	Taste/tasty
Seek	Tune in	Stroke	Stagnant	Tasteful
Shadow	Vibrate	Thump	Stank	Teeth (get into)
Shine	Voice	Tingle	Success (smell)	Tip of tongue
Sparkle	Volume	Velvet	Trace of	Tongue tied
Stare	Whisper	Warm	Whiff	Zest
Visualise	Yap	Weight		

If this fires you up, sounds like something you would like to pursue, or is clearly an avenue of development for you, then you might look further into the concept of NLP or Neuro Linguistic Programming. Using sensory language to describe situations will certainly have those neurons lighting up and synapses sparking instantly.

There's a balance to be found which may take some practise and effort. We don't want to be so literal as to convey dry information that won't be remembered, nor do we want to turn our story into something so flowery and descriptive that we quickly lose our logical, analytical listeners and everyone else gets lost along the way. As with everything we want to master, it's about giving it a go, calibrating and changing what didn't work.

K.I.S.S!

This acronym is sometimes known as 'Keep It Simple Stupid', but I prefer '**Keep It Simple** yet **Stylish**'. We may have been blessed with a high level of education, passionate and articulate parents or we may simply like eating dictionaries for breakfast. Our audience however will likely stem from varying backgrounds and levels of education, so we want to keep our language simple.

When storytelling for business, watch out for jargon and TLAs (which stands for Three Letter Acronyms, using the first letter of each word instead of the whole word). Complex or function/department-specific language might not be understood by everyone in the organisation and may also come across as elitist, so aim to re-read your story through the eyes of the newest recruit and make the necessary changes.

Boundaries of Language

Be aware of using colloquial and colourful language in your stories. There is a fine line between endearing the audience to you through familiarity or informality and instantly turning them off you because you went a step too far.

Only you will know what constitutes an acceptable level of informal communication between you and your audience. If you have a smidgen of doubt, run your story by a few people first to gauge their response. If you don't find the right balance your audience may vote with their feet.

Always follow the golden rule: If in doubt, leave it out!

In Summary

The language you use in your story can make the difference between your presentation being interesting or being captivating. It's like using the freshest, most fragrant, colourful and highest quality deli-market ingredients in your recipe as opposed to the cheapest, blandest supermarket stock. Your audience will know the difference, even though they may not be able to quite put their finger on it.

It's not until you listen to a story with this newly acquired or refreshed knowledge that you will be able to distinguish, with an expert ear, those people who have masterfully constructed their story to appeal to varying learning preferences, senses and personality types.

The easier it looks, the more practice you know the storyteller has put into weaving magic so that you, the audience, can be captivated. Listen out for sensory language in the next presentations you hear, to get it well and truly fixed onto your radar.

Have fun and be creative.

A Sprinkling of Magic

Thoughts, Ideas and Reminders so far

Chapter Six

Storytelling and Personality Type

CHAPTER 6. STORYTELLING AND PERSONALITY TYPE

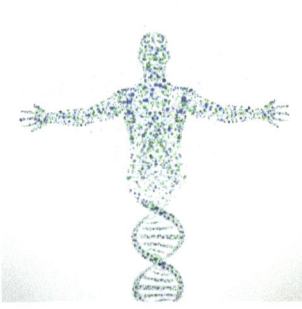

When telling our story, we want to appeal to all differing personality preferences, so if we become familiar with some of the key differences in personality type and consciously include messages and language that appeal to them, then we can further increase our ability to influence.

I could write a book solely about personality type as it is an area of fascination for me, however for the context of storytelling, I'll distil it into a few key points.

Consider the descriptions below and then think about your audience. If you know them well and have a good idea of where their preferences lie, aim to tailor your story accordingly. Deliver your story according to their preferences rather than yours.

> **Introverts versus Extraverts** – Introverts tend to be the more active listeners of the two preferences as they are more reflective. They listen, think, reflect, then may or may not speak. Introverts may appear to you as passive listeners and may even come across as disconnected or disassociated. What's more likely to be happening is that they are experiencing the story and interpreting it internally.

> There may be a section of the story that you would anticipate emotion to be displayed from your audience, but you may not get this from the introverts. For an introverted audience it's important to include plenty of pauses.

> I am naturally extraverted, so I have to make a conscious effort when my audience consists primarily of introverts, to slow down the pace, speak less loudly and limit my hand gestures. I speak much more deliberately and increase the pauses.

> Extraverts on the other hand tend to be more visually engaged as listeners. You will see them nodding their heads in agreement, contributing with 'aha's' and other little affirmative signs, and they will be more expressive, reacting immediately to your message.

> It's much easier to know if an extravert isn't listening because their body language says it all. Maintain frequent eye contact to keep extraverts engaged and ask tag questions (see Secret Magic Ingredients in Chapter 10).

> **Practical versus Creative** – If you know that your audience members have a practical bias, make sure to include plenty of facts and use down to earth practical language. Check the logical sequence and restrict the use of metaphor but don't leave out altogether.

Metaphors, quotes, poems and speech excerpts are more the language of the creative preference, so this is where you can wax lyrical with your sensory language and highly descriptive anecdotes and tales.

➢ **Big Picture versus Detail** – While some people like to hear about the key salient points of a story, others prefer to go right into the nitty gritty of detail. This can be a hard one to find common ground on, but is very important to consider.

If you are a big picture storyteller, then you may leave a detail-oriented audience feeling frustrated, leaving too much out and preventing them from getting the meaning in the message. The converse is also true in that an audience of big picture listeners will bore and tire easily if there's too much detail. You can tell by seeing that glazed-over look – that's if you can see their eyes before they close them!

A good rule of thumb is to start with the big picture and move quickly on to some detail about what is to be covered then, if necessary, return to the big picture to complete your opening message.

➢ **Rational (head first) versus Values Driven (heart first)** – Those with a preference for logic, analysis and rational thinking will be looking for validation of any points that you make. For example, if you quote any studies or experiments in your story, be prepared to back your data up with a valid source.

If your audience is primarily rational, you are probably best to keep the emotional elements to a minimum (unless of course this is your key message) as they may feel uncomfortable and distance themselves.

Those with a preference for being values-based tend to think first with their heart and then check in with their heads. A story devoid of emotion will not sink in or connect with these preferences at all, so be sure to include something about the character's feelings and responses.

➢ **Structured versus Spontaneous** – People with a preference for structure will want the story to have a clear beginning, middle and end. They'll be asking themselves *"what happens next?"* and *"what happens after that?"* as they have a preference for sequential thinking.

Spontaneous and flexible sorts love to be taken on a surprise journey with twists and turns* on every corner, so the more you digress and come up with surprise plots, the more you will delight them. Again, this is a delicate balance to find, so aim to cover a bit of both if you don't know your audience and their preferences so well.

*There is an advanced form of storytelling that involves opening up multiple stories and closing them down again in reverse order. This concept is known as 'open loop metaphor' or 'nested loops' and is used often by therapists, coaches and master storytellers.

If you would like to study some of these masters, then search for footage of Ronnie Corbett (of the British comedy duo The Two Ronnies); specifically footage of his storytelling from a chair. Others include comedians Billy Connolly and Victoria Wood, and the most famous open loop storyteller of all is hypnotherapist Milton Erikson.

After your Story - If you want to initiate discussion following your story, be aware of who your practical listeners are and let them come to the discussion in their own time. It may be that they take longer to make the connections (depending on the subtlety of the story of course) otherwise they may not get it at all.

Those with a preference for creativity may actively initiate the discussion and subconsciously lead those with a practical preference to interpret the learnings - or not.

Notes about the Personality Types and Characteristics of my Audience

In Summary

You can't please all of the people all of the time, but by taking into account the different personalities in your audience, you have a much better chance of pleasing most of the people most of the time.

The more in tune you are with your audience and the more you can read their signals of engagement, the better you will be able to tweak and refine your story to their preferred ways of learning and listening, which embeds your message at a deeper construct level.

Chapter Seven

Storytelling in Business and Public Speaking

Chapter 7. Storytelling in Business and Public Speaking

"Storytelling is the single most powerful tool in a leader's toolkit."
Dr Howard Gardner, Harvard University Professor, author of 'Changing Minds'

By now you are well aware that storytelling takes many different forms. If you are a manager or leader in business, I wouldn't advocate that you get the board members around the table and kick off with: *"Once upon a time, in a faraway land"*!

Great leaders are effective communicators, or certainly need to be! If you think about the role of storytelling in indigenous cultures, it is usually the elders and shaman who gather everyone around to share their insight and wisdom and who pass on the rich history and culture through story. They also pass on the laws of the people, the culture, the expected norms and the consequences of going against those norms, and they do so in the form of parable and sharing their own journeys through life.

The greater percentage of business leaders by their nature are logical, rational and analytical (as opposed to subjective, emotional and metaphorical), and so may at first be uncomfortable with storytelling as a concept for communication. We also know however that this is the age of the emotionally intelligent leader, and there is a need for stronger connection between a leader and their people.

Stories are the bridges that leaders can use to build powerful connections, demonstrate their humanness, vulnerability and strength and the 'I'm just like you' analogy. They can also use stories to inspire in challenging times.

At first you may think that there aren't many stories inside of you, however it's just a case of accessing those parts of the brain that hold certain memories and, once you start, you'll be amazed at the volume, quality and depth of stories you have to share.

Remember from previous chapters that a story can be as simple as recounting an experience or using an example. It doesn't have to be complex.

As soon as you move from 'third party' to 'authentic me' – you have a captive audience.

A Sprinkling of Magic

Classic stories that reside in leaders' heads can answer the questions that many of us can learn and develop from. Example questions include:

- How did you get started?
- What were the greatest lessons from your earlier career and how have they impacted the way you lead/run your business today?
- What was your biggest failure or mistake, what impact did it have and what lesson did you learn from it?
- Who was your most inspiring boss and why?
- What did you learn from your most challenging boss?
- How have you dealt with failure in your career?
- How do you motivate yourself on a daily basis and in challenging times?
- What strategies do you have for prioritising and decision-making and how did you develop them?
- What's the greatest risk you've ever taken and what was the result?
- What's the most innovative project or idea you have ever embarked upon?
- If you had your time again, what would you do differently?
- If you could work in any industry (other than this one) what would it be and why?
- Did you ever doubt your ability and how did you overcome the doubt?
- What's the craziest thing you have ever done in business?
- What story from business has had the greatest impact on you?
- Who do you look to as mentors and examples of exceptional business leaders?
- Tell us about the biggest goal you achieved and how you went about it?
- Who do you mentor or coach and how has it helped them grow?
- What's the best piece of advice you've ever received and what action did you take?
- What's the most inspiring biography you have read and why did it inspire you?

See also the question table in 'Your Stories' in Chapter 8.

A Sprinkling of Magic

One of the most inspiring bosses I ever had was a master of metaphor and storytelling. He used stories to bring us together as a management team, to inspire us to think about what was achievable and to instil in us a sense of pride and ownership.

"One bite at a time"

I used to work for an international Internet Service Provider in the 'dot com' boom period. We were executing a US$2 billion European expansion plan and our business plans were changing daily.

I felt completely overwhelmed at one point and went to see my boss Mike for some help and advice. His opening question was "*How do you eat an elephant, Clare?*" I wasn't very impressed and thought he was teasing me for being a vegetarian. I believe my response was quite rude, which he thankfully ignored, then he proceeded to tell me that the answer was "*One bite at a time*".

We then spent the next hour together trawling through all of my projects and likening them to the trunk, ears, face, body, legs, until we reached the tail, and I left his office feeling so much more in control. The elephant metaphor has stayed with me all these years.

This is a simple example yet one that was highly effective for me as I was able to make the comparison. I subsequently used the same metaphor to lead my team in times of stress.

Another of Mike's favourite terms was 'jungle arithmetic'. Finance and budgeting were probably not my greatest strengths, and he used to ask me to imagine that I was in the jungle without access to a calculator or computer. We would then go through the figures in a very rough way, but it had the desired effect of making me comfortable first and feeling competent before we needed to drill down into the more complex financial details.

Your stories and analogies don't always have to be complex; they just need to convey the most effective message at the most appropriate time. How might you be able to use simple metaphor and analogy to help someone who might be struggling?

The role of Social Media in Storytelling for Business

We tend to think of storytelling as a face-to-face medium but social media has opened up the gamut to appeal to a much broader audience. Never before has mass media advertising become so affordable or so instant – all it takes is your imagination and creativity.

You may already be telling stories through case studies and success stories to be found in your marketing literature and possibly on your website, however, are you making the most of...

Blogs and Articles

If you have a quick win with your business, you are able, with permission of course, to post this directly to your blog or communications page. Now a blog doesn't have to be perfectly written and structured – you can break all the rules here. What you should include is the simple framework of:

1. The problem your client had
2. The solution you developed or offered
3. The positive result or outcome

Podcasting

Podcasts were made for story! It's not expensive but it can be time-consuming. Be selective about who you choose to invite on your podcast (this is your brand remember) and invite them to share their tales from the trenches as well as their successes.

LinkedIn

Of all the current social media sites, LinkedIn is best suited for building business to business relationships. You can also join industry specific professional groups and share your success stories or better still, have linking buttons from your blog to all the other social media sites where you are represented.

Social Networks (Facebook, Instagram, Tik Tok etc.)

All of the above sites are ideal media for you to grow prospect and customer loyalty through your stories. Make sure though that for these media that you have an attractive headline, and your story is succinct and compelling as our attention spans are increasingly diminishing.

When you make storytelling integral to your internal and external communications, you are endearing yourself to ALL of your stakeholders and it's not going to cost you the earth.

Conveying Your Message with Metaphors and Analogies

Being able to liken your business situation to something comparable is an effective storytelling method in business. This ticks all the boxes of storytelling in that it captures the imagination of your people, each having their own interpretation yet understanding the goal or vision, and it opens up avenues for innovation and creativity.

Beware however of overusing metaphors and analogies and losing people, or of continually using the same metaphor so that it becomes boring. For example, sporting analogies tend to be overused in business, but we can still use them if they are **topical, specific and relevant**. Here are a few examples:

Generic Analogy	Specific Analogy
Sailing – we need to chart our course, make sure that everyone is in the same boat, understands the destination and can get back on track when we veer off course	The Clipper round the World yacht race open to everyone. The America's Cup The Sydney to Hobart Race
Exploring – you need to stick your neck out and explore new territory and deal with challenges head on, preparing to be flexible	The story of Ernest Shackleton and the Imperial Trans Antarctic Expedition of 1914-1917 where his ship *'Endurance'* was stuck in pack ice. Shackleton's goal changed to saving his men, which he achieved
Adventuring – project preparation, trust, teamwork, milestones, goals, expanding comfort zones, facing challenges, persistence, etc.	Sir Edmund Hillary and Sherpa Tenzing Norgay as the first to conquer Mount Everest in 1953. The story of climbers Joe Simpson and Simon Yates as portrayed in the documentary 'Touching the Void'
Practical Optimism – being able to endure and bounce back from challenge, disappointment and rejection and win through in the end	Viktor Frankl's 3 years in various concentration camps in WWII and his triumph as told in his book 'Man's Search for Meaning'

Additional Applications of Stories

Here's a simple list to provoke thinking around different applications:

- To inspire creativity
- To build trust and credibility
- To fire the imagination and encourage lateral thinking
- To extrapolate systems, processes, themes and ideas
- To help embed values
- To connect with all learning preferences
- To share history and tradition
- To challenge current beliefs and attitudes
- To provide alternative perspectives
- To bring another dimension to learning
- To liven up meetings
- To communicate a mission and vision
- To enable and facilitate change
- To anticipate and address resistance
- To push us beyond our comfort zone
- To bring thinking into alignment
- To hand down cultural traditions
- To address issues and challenges in a respectful way
- To gain permission to continue a dialogue
- To show authenticity, openness and vulnerability
- To elicit a common theme or issue
- To convey identity and culture
- To engage and engender loyalty and pride
- To illustrate a principle
- To change the current mood
- To encourage us to dream
- To add humour to experience
- To honour individual uniqueness and interpretation
- To differentiate yourself as a communicator and leader

A Sprinkling of Magic

Guidelines and Tips for finding Analogies and Metaphors

> ➤ **Look to nature** – natural phenomena such as icebergs, volcanoes, storms, rainbows, avalanches, tsunamis and bushfires

>> I frequently use icebergs as a metaphor for personality, with behaviours and skills being above the surface or on the waterline, and underneath, the deeper complexities of our attitudes, values, beliefs and identity

> ➤ **Look to natural wonders and great feats** – Pyramids of Giza, Great Wall of China, Barrier Reef, Stonehenge, Taj Mahal, Machu Picchu, Angkor Wat, Aurora Borealis (Northern Lights) to name just a few

>> What can we learn from nature, phenomenal projects and teamwork that we can apply in life and business today?

> ➤ **Look to history and ancient civilization** - Greek Mythology, the Romans, Incas, Mayans, Aztecs, Chinese, Egyptians and many more

>> How did these ancient 'possibility thinkers' live, organise themselves and achieve the impossible?

> ➤ **Look to evolution** – this is another simple yet powerful metaphor that can be applied to almost anything Remember to be culturally sensitive though as it's not everyone's belief

There are many ways to depict evolution these days!

> ➤ **Look to the animal world** – extraordinary animal journeys such as salmon, birds migrating, green turtles, wildebeest, etc. Animals and insects that make great teams such as geese, ants, bees, wolves, huskies and meerkats

Metamorphosis is a powerful metaphor for change (though sometimes poorly used or overused). Look at how a spider spins its web for a metaphor for persistence (you can find the story of Robert the Bruce, King of Scotland and the spider in 101 Inspiring Stories for Business and Life), or look to the cicada for patience (do the research and make up your own mind)

- ➢ **Look to endurance sport** – Tour de France, Paris to Dakar rally, Marathon de Sables, Hawaii Ironman Championships. What is it about these competitors that keep them going through the most excruciating pain or continual dangers?

- ➢ **Look to the art world** – works of art (e.g. is your business more of an Andy Warhol than a Leonardo Da Vinci?), the statue of David, the Sistine Chapel, the Terracotta Army, the Mona Lisa. Works of art are great metaphors for innovation, creativity and uniqueness

- ➢ **Look to the media** – now it's on your radar you will find a plethora of metaphors and analogies in newspapers, on TV, in movies, books and magazines

- ➢ **Look to innovation** – there are a plethora of stories of innovation that came out of the Covid era, and you must be living under a rock to be unaware of stories of impact of robotics and artificial intelligence

Other great metaphors and analogies include recipes, topical issues such as the environment and climate change, extinction of species and inventions (good and bad)

The only thing that can limit you is your imagination!

My Ideas for Analogies and Metaphors

Guidelines and Tips for using Analogies and Metaphors

> ***Do your research*** – if some of the ideas mentioned appeal to you, then research them as there is a story to be found behind them all. The more you research the more you will find to share and inspire

> ***Be topical*** – use recent events such as natural phenomena (volcano eruptions, meteors, planet alignments etc.) Scan the news to find topical openings for your stories

> ***Personalise*** – if you are creating a story or metaphor for a client at a speaking engagement, find a way to personalise it so its meaning has greater depth. This will also endear you to the client as you have made the extra effort

> ***Be culturally and geographically relevant and respectful*** – e.g. if your audience isn't North American, steer clear of baseball or ice hockey analogies

I once worked for a company whose headquarters were in another continent. We were based in Europe and they rolled out a new product based on the 'Mission Impossible' theme and made two key mistakes:

Firstly, the film wasn't due to be released in the UK and Europe until three months after product launch (and the DVDs were not compatible anyway). Secondly, they wanted the management team to dress up as gangsters, which would have gone down culturally like a lead balloon with our reserved Brits!

> ***Look and Listen*** - be on the lookout for juicy bits of news or conversations that make for good metaphors and analogies. Listen also for metaphors that the people around you are using so that you can pick up on them and utilise them where appropriate

Once your brain is activated (using its Reticular Activating System or RAS), you will start to see and hear metaphors and analogies everywhere, in the media, in advertising, when reading or just overhearing conversations.

Think about keeping a notebook (paper or digital) to jot ideas down, as just one small idea could grow into a magical metaphor that inspires your people to listen and take action.

In Summary

We are surrounded by rich material to develop our stories, both from within and without. Though it takes extra effort in compiling your story, the payoff will be evident in how clearly the message and the meanings are received.

The more you can customise your metaphors, the more deeply they will be ingrained in the subconscious minds of your listeners and the greater effect they will have.

Chapter Eight

Sourcing Examples for Business and Speaker Stories

Chapter 8. Sourcing Examples for Business and Speaker Stories

We know that being able to use examples of what we are looking to achieve can really help illustrate a point, provide benchmarks for best practice (both good and bad) and motivate people to believe that goals are achievable.

There are many role models from history that I use. In my emotional resilience workshops, I run a quiz called 'The World's Greatest Bouncers'. There are 18 pictures of which participants must guess the names, and I read out a short biography of each and why they deserve to be on 'The World's Greatest Bouncer' list. This is often cited as one of the most memorable and inspiring sections of the workshop.

I am always looking for role models to both emulate and avoid in many categories and would encourage you to continue your research and maintain relevance and/or currency. Here are a few for starters:

Company/Person	Examples of Excellence and Success
3M	Innovation – Post It Note story and bootlegging time
Apple	Product innovation, knowing your core purpose (WHY you are in business)
Brendan Grimshaw – Brit who bought an island in the Seychelles	Values, integrity, contribution to the planet
Emirates Airlines	Exceptional Customer Service
Flight Centre	Employee engagement and culture – families and tribes
Glastonbury Music Festival UK	Organisation and customer experience on a grand scale
Honda	Stakeholder Relationship Management – supplier engagement
IKEA	Culture – employees are members of the IKEA family = IKEANS
Innocent Drinks	Customer experience, innovation, risk, cheeky informality
Johnson & Johnson	The Transparent Organisation with a credo
Malala Yousafzai	Pakistani Education activist, shot by the Taliban at 15 years of age

A Sprinkling of Magic

Company/Person	Examples of Excellence and Success
Mastercard, Johnson & Johnson, Apple, Cisco	Commitment to Diversity & Inclusion
Nordstrom	Whatever it takes to delight the customer
Patagonia Clothing	Values – commitment to the environment and employees
Richard Branson	Entrepreneurship and possibility thinking, values and culture
Roger Bannister	Achieving what was 'scientifically proven' to be impossible
Southwest Airlines	Culture and customer experience. Even their stock symbol is LUV!
Suni Williams and Butch Wilmore (2 NASA astronauts stuck in space)	Optimism, reframing challenges as opportunities, resilience
Toyota	TPS (Total Production System) Lean Manufacturing
Turia Pitt	Australian bushfire survivor and role model for resilience
Unilever	Commitment to sustainability
Zappos	10 committable core values and culture focused on delivering happiness
Company	**Examples of Mediocrity and Failure**
Enron	Values and incongruence
Fyre Festival (2017)	Over promising and under delivering
Kodak, Blockbuster, Borders, Nokia	Failure to adapt, complacency
Lehman Bros	Subprime loan scandal
Sports Direct (UK)	Working conditions in overseas factories
Volkswagen	Emissions Test cheating

A Sprinkling of Magic

Take your People to the Movies

Have you ever come into work in the morning and a colleague just had to tell you about an amazing film they had seen that really touched them to the core? We can use films as stories and in the same way that a story lays the foundation for conversation, so does a great inspirational movie.

I have been part of a team that came together for an after-hours evening of inspiration. We had some nibbles and drinks then watched a film and chatted about the key points afterwards. (The film was 'Touching the Void'). We all had a different insight into this cliff-hanger of a documentary and its message, and each manager's input was valid in its own right. We then took those key lessons and embedded them into our own personal and professional development.

As you read this, what films are coming to mind that have inspired you? Below is a list of what, in my opinion, are exceptionally inspiring films. You will have your own thoughts and opinions, so I won't share my interpretation; rather I will leave you with my suggested list of movies to watch and I would encourage you to keep a record of your own favourites in the open spaces.

Movie	Key Themes and Points to note
Braveheart	
The Bucket List	
Chariots of Fire	
Dead Poets Society	
The Help	
Hidden Figures	

A Sprinkling of Magic

Movie	Key Themes and Points to note
The Imitation Game	
Inside Out	
The Intouchables	
Invictus	
To Kill a Mockingbird	
The King's Speech	
Little Miss Sunshine	
On the Basis of Sex	
Patch Adams	
In Pursuit of Happyness	
Slumdog Millionaire	
Touching the Void	
UP!	
The World's Fastest Indian	

A Sprinkling of Magic

Other Peoples' Stories

I studied the Foundations of Positive Psychology with Tal Ben Shahar, lecturer at LPS College, Penn State University, one of the most popular courses at Harvard. Tal shared something that really struck a chord with me; he said that **the best self-development books are biographies and autobiographies**. I couldn't agree more.

When I study the lives of people who achieved the extraordinary, it inspires me to action. I can see myself in their predicaments and realise that mostly it is our limiting beliefs that hold us back, rather than external conditions. They also take me back to being the hero as mentioned in the beginning of the book.

Here are some biographies and memoirs that I would encourage you to read:

- Anita Roddick – Business as Unusual (The Body Shop)
- Anne Frank – The Diary of Anne Frank
- Eddie Jaku – The Happiest Man on Earth
- Ghandi – My Experiments with Truth
- Michelle Obama – Becoming
- Nelson Mandela – Long Walk to Freedom
- Paul Kalanithi – When Breath becomes Air
- Richard Branson – Losing my Virginity
- Yvon Chouinard – Let my People go Surfing (Patagonia)

YOUR Stories

Whether you know it or not, you are full of amazing stories! We are all full of amazing stories and it's just a case of extracting them. When I first started running team development workshops, I was shy about sharing my stories with people. It wasn't until it happened inadvertently, and I received the response that I did, that I realised the power of my own stories.

The three most respected qualities (you have to trust me on this because I can't find the source) of a speaker and storyteller are **authenticity**, **vulnerability** and **spontaneity**. When you are prepared to give of yourself and show your humanness, this is when you will connect the most with your audience.

Let me give you an example. I am an avid fan of Ingham and Luft's Johari Window model, and I use it to illustrate the importance and implications of developing self-awareness. The second pane of the window is called the 'blind spot' and looks at information others know about us but that we don't know about ourselves.

A Sprinkling of Magic

I use a story from my days as a manager in the hospitality industry to illustrate my then rather large blind spot. I was managing a team of receptionists for a large hotel chain, and I was extremely proud of my team and considered myself to be a good manager.

Have a read of this story and be aware of your conscious and subconscious responses:

> *Picture this: I'm at the typewriter (yes, it was before word processing came to the masses) typing another memo. My nails are almost flying off as my fingers hit the keys with my 'tut tut tuts' in sync with my 'tap tap taps' on the keyboard. My boss asks me what I'm typing the memo for and I respond, "It doesn't matter how often I remind the girls (the team was all female), they consistently fail to obtain passport details from guests wanting to cash travellers cheques."*
>
> *At that moment, Felicity, our trainee receptionist, a beautiful young girl from the Welsh countryside, popped her head round the door, looked at me with her huge brown doe eyes and said, as a tear trickled down her cheek, "Clare, it doesn't matter what we do or don't do because nothing we do can ever match up to the standards you set us"- and with that she went back to attend to a guest.*
>
> *OUCH! I felt like someone had just dropped a medicine ball on my heart. I was totally unaware of my reputation with the team. I found out that I was secretly known as the Memo Queen and there were competitions between the girls as to how many memos per week they would find in their pigeon holes!*
>
> *I went home and took a good hard look at myself and my management style and made a decision to face up to the girls the next day and arrange to get together and talk about what we wanted collectively as a team. From that day forward my management style changed beyond recognition. I became more consultative, more trusting and always remembered to give genuine praise and honest feedback where it was due.*

Can you see how this story illustrates a theoretical point and brings it to life? I was prepared to let people know that I stuffed up. This is how you can become so much more engaging as a leader and a speaker, when you are prepared to disclose and divulge.

Brainstorming and Extraction

So how do you source your stories? Our brains are like a huge hard drive and contain many databases. We just need a way to be able to get back to those dusty old filing cabinets and retrieve the records. In NLP stories are called 'reference experiences' and, in addition to previous prompter questions in Chapter 7, I have put together additional prompters and triggers that will help you to re-access that database and find examples that can become your signature stories. You'll be surprised if not amazed at the amount of material you have that can be crafted into a memorable story with a meaning in its message.

Can you remember a time when … (Just jot down notes on the right-hand side as and when they come up), you can embellish later.

Trigger/Question	**Reference Experience**
You not only achieved a goal – you absolutely blitzed it	
You underperformed beyond your worst expectations	
You took yourself way out of your comfort zone and it paid off immensely	
You took yourself way out of your comfort zone and ended up in pure panic	
You made gross assumptions, with consequences	
You wanted something so badly, you never once doubted that you wouldn't get it	
You were totally 'in flow', in the zone, time disappeared, you felt masterful	
You were so emotional that the decisions you made were irrational and had consequences	
You were empathic and actively and respectfully listened to someone and it resulted in …	
You took a major risk and it paid off	
You were afraid to fail and missed a significant opportunity	

Trigger/Question	Reference Experience
You faced up to someone and had 'the real conversation' and it resulted in …	
Your intuition kicked in and you just knew … and acted on your gut instinct	
You made a major decision based on your values	
You made a decision that compromised your values, and it resulted in…	
You decided to leave a relationship, unsure of the consequences and it resulted in …	
You decided to stay in a relationship, unsure of the consequences and it resulted in …	
You stuck to your guns and the impact it had was…	
You did something so silly that you wanted the floor to swallow you up (but you can laugh about it now!)	
You received a piece of advice that you acted upon and it turned out to be gold	
You developed a new and resourceful habit and did it by……	
You made a judgement call on someone and they turned out to be completely different	
You decided to let go of the outcome of a decision and ….	
You were so proud you thought that your heart would burst	

Additional ways to Source your Stories

Let yourself be interviewed – a good friend interviewed me last year and I was amazed at what I could remember and the value these experiences could add to my message. Amber would start with a question similar to the ones in previous tables then drill a little further down to elicit my feelings, more detail and hence more contrast.

Ask friends and family – ask family members and close friends what their most vivid memories of you are and why – you'll be surprised at what they know and their perspectives.

Ask for peer feedback – you might be pleasantly surprised at what people come up with and it's also an opportunity for your peers to feed back to you those areas that might be in your blind spot. Be kind to yourself though and start by asking about your strengths.

Re-read or write your résumé – by doing this you are taking your mind back to those experiences and accessing specific areas of memory. Allow yourself to daydream about the jobs you have had in the past, what the key challenges were and how you overcame them, what the major wins and achievements were and why they were successful.

Reflect on your life's turning points – I used to live close to Australia Zoo and, in honour of Steve Irwin, I like to call these 'CRIKEY' moments! Think about a chapter in your life where you had an epiphany, a revelation or a change of mind/heart that had a major impact and write about it.

Journal – if you have kept a journal or diary in the past, re-read it as it's a great memory jogger. If you haven't it's not too late to start and what will happen is that as you describe new experiences, memories of similar experiences will pop back into your head.

Sharing your stories with a little Caution - as much as we may love stories, be aware that they need to have a purpose and be used with volition. I have witnessed too many speakers use story after story after story and, in isolation, they could have been so powerful, but layer upon layer for the sake of it could result in you losing your audience and their respect for you.

If you want to share your story and it's been a challenging journey, make sure you are fully ready, willing and most importantly able to share without breaking down or re-associating into the pain. Your intent may be to inspire people but, unless you can keep your composure, your story may end up having the opposite effect. It's a fine balance as you don't want to come across as dissociated either.

Choose, use and tell your stories wisely

Chapter Nine

Learning Styles
An introduction to the 4MAT

Chapter 9. Learning Styles – An Introduction to the 4MAT

You want to captivate as many of your audience members as possible, right? In which case it helps to understand the variety of ways in which people process and perceive information i.e. the differing learning styles that people will have a preference for.

Just as with personality, we are able to learn in all four ways, it's just that we will have one or two dominant natural preferences.

The 4MAT system was developed by schoolteacher Dr Bernice McCarthy and I have found it invaluable in structuring all my presentations, workshops and stories. I don't always use the 4MAT as a sequential way to construct my story; I read through it as if I'm each of the four preferences and think – will this appeal to me?

WHY? *"Why should I be interested in this?"* - **Imaginative learners** seek personal involvement, meaning and connections in what they learn. They prefer the big picture, will form links and patterns and use their imagination

WHAT? *"What is this about, what will we cover?"* – **Practical learners** seek facts and information, formulate ideas and think them through. They like structure and process and need time to reflect

HOW? *"How does it work, how can I use it?"* - **Enthusiastic learners** learn by doing, they're the common-sense tactile learners and want to get stuck in by building, experimenting and applying ideas. They are very hands on and will get bored if there is too much theory

WHAT IF? *"What if we did it this way, would it work?"* - **Dynamic learners** learn by exploring, seeking possibilities, self-discovery and trial and error. They are often unaware of timescales - it's about getting it right in the end.

A simple example of using this as an introduction to a story might be:

"Have you ever jumped into a situation feet first only to end up wearing the consequences? I'd like to share with you a story about how I almost wrecked a professional relationship and how I used the experience to change the way I handle conflict, so that if ever I was in a similar situation, I could almost guarantee a win/win outcome.

Would you like to hear my story?"

Let's break it down:

WHY - *Have you ever jumped into a situation feet first only to end up wearing the consequences?*

WHAT - *I'd like to share with you a story about how I almost wrecked a professional relationship, and*

HOW - *how I used the experience to change the way I handle conflict so that,*

WHAT IF - *if ever I was in a similar situation, I could almost guarantee a win/win outcome.*

Would you like to hear my story?

Can you see how everyone is catered for in four clear and simple sentences? This easy and effective method for ensuring that all learning styles are included has been one of the greatest finds for me in storytelling and business in general.

Whenever I open a workshop, a speech, a story or write a proposal, I use the 4MAT to develop the framework. I just repeat to myself - 'WHY, WHAT, HOW, WHAT IF!' Please don't underestimate its simplicity – it is powerful. For more information about the 4MAT you can visit aboutlearning.com

Jot down the current way you prepare to tell or introduce a story

A Sprinkling of Magic

Consider re-phrasing your opening using the 4MAT

1. WHY	2. WHAT

3. HOW	4. WHAT IF

Chapter Ten

The Secret Magic Ingredients

CHAPTER 10. THE SECRET MAGIC INGREDIENTS

Whilst we have already covered many of the major components of storytelling, this is about adding an extra special sprinkling of magic, that 'je ne sais quoi' that, when practised, will endear your audience to you even though they might not quite know why. If this were a recipe, this section would be all the secret herbs and spices that make your dish stand out from the rest and that the chef refuses to share.

You have the material, and you have an audience; we now want to refine the delivery so that we transform listeners into captivated fans. Let's start.

1. Preparing for your Audience

Earlier on I shared with you my childhood example of the radio show *'Listen with Mother'*. When the presenter Daphne Oxenford started with *"Are you sitting comfortably? Then I'll begin"*, I used to talk back to the radio and shout *"YES I AM!"* Daphne was preparing us to shift into listening mode.

Looking back with the skills I have now, I would shuffle and settle when she asked the question and I believe that my brain, once conditioned to this stimulus response mechanism, would fire up its storylistening neurology which included:

- Moving my body into a comfortable position that I could remain in for the duration of the story (or as long as a kid can stay focused!)

- Focusing my primary sense to auditory (often closing me eyes)

- Shutting out extraneous noise and distractions

- Firing up the creative parts of my brain to light up my imagination, visual cortex and pattern making programs

And all without having a clue as to what I was doing.

It is a rule of thumb from cognitive scientists (cited George P Lakoff) that up to 95% of our behaviour happens at an unconscious level. Think about it – do you tell your stomach to produce acids and enzymes to start digesting your food? Do you tell your heart to beat X times per minute or your lungs to expand and contract by X%?

To use the iceberg metaphor, it's all happening below the surface. The same goes for our behaviour and thinking patterns. What you see is NOT what you get; we are complex creatures with differing attitudes, beliefs, values and personalities.

When we think of our audience, what is it we want them to be thinking as they listen to our story? What is it that we want them to take away as the strongest message? And what mood do we want to set that will have them connected with us and open to listening?

"Be in the state that you want to create!" This is about being totally congruent with and experiencing the mood or attitude we want to instil in our audience. For example, if your story is about making and learning from mistakes, be open, honest, humble and willing to share. If your story is about building confidence, stand tall, project your voice and emphasise eye contact.

If you want to instil curiosity in your audience, then make sure you have an air of curiosity about you and that your story builds curiosity and suspense as you go. You can use the reflector gesture (see Deliberate Gestures) to create the state of contemplation and curiosity.

2. Mastering your Delivery

Your Voice

Your voice is your main vehicle for delivery and can make the difference between mediocrity and magic, so use it wisely and look after it well.

Take care of your Voice - if your story is going to take longer than 10 minutes to tell and you don't want to break rapport by taking a drink, make sure your voice is well lubricated before you start. This means avoiding coffee, salt and alcohol before you speak. You can improve lubrication by drinking warm (not hot) water and honey and there are also throat sprays available over the counter. If you prefer cold water, make sure it's not too chilled as this will impede your voice quality.

Voice Quality - you want to be able to use your voice like a musical instrument, i.e. have range, tone and timbre which adds a rich quality to the sound of your voice. The best way to develop this is to read your story into a voice recorder and listen back to it. Exaggerate at first to practise contrast.

Become consciously aware of where you might be slipping into monotone (which is a sure way to send your audience to sleep), or if you find that you are dropping off at the end of your sentences (or going up as many Australians do), as this could irritate the audience as they listen more to your inflections than to the story.

A Sprinkling of Magic

I am a huge fan of a very well-known spiritual medic who originates from the East, though I sometimes fall asleep listening to his podcasts as he has a certain tone that just puts me into trance. I even have an audiobook of his about dealing with insomnia and haven't ever reached the end because I've fallen asleep!

Listen to some audiobooks and pick out what it is about the storyteller's voice that is adding quality to the delivery. Is there a cadence in the voice? - i.e. a variation of rise and fall, high and low, soft and strong. Is there a variation in speed and volume? Is there light and shade that provides a contrast? Listen to the radio to a professional, well-oiled DJ and hone your listening skills to voice nuances.

Every little change you make will hit a mark in the listener's mind, fire up the neurology and have them listening attentively again.

Volume – this may take a little practice, but you don't want to be so quiet that your audience has to strain to hear you; neither do you want to be bellowing at them. I always check in with my audience before presenting and have learned how to use a microphone correctly.

If your group is small and intimate, then you probably won't need voice amplification but if you have more than 30 people or are in a large room, it definitely pays to use a microphone. If you want to use hand gestures, then consider a lapel or head mic as you may be restricted with a handheld (and may be using a slide advancer in the other hand).

Cadence and Tonality – it's a good idea to record yourself telling a story and then listening specifically for these qualities. Does your voice rise and fall with specific sentences or words? Can you add a soft 'sing-song' lilting tone or a deeper sombre tone depending on the nature of the message?

Do you have a tendency to go up at the end of every sentence or even drop off the last few words? Your cadence and tonality are the golden nuggets that will make the difference between your audience listening politely and being enthralled.

Think about children's stories and practise them again to exaggerate the richness and diversity that you have been gifted with, in your voice.

Dialect, Accent and Enunciation – you may be telling your story in a language other than your native tongue or have a regional dialect or accent. Don't try to change this because it is who you are and is probably a core strength. It may also distract you and you might come over as insincere or forced. If your accent is strong, remember to speak a little slower.

Enunciation is important in storytelling as listeners can switch off if they don't catch all your words and do not have the opportunity to ask you to repeat yourself. Be aware also of the speed of your storytelling, pronounce all the words and try not to speak too quickly.

A Sprinkling of Magic

Your Breathing

When you're telling a story you are using your lungs for longer. All that change in tonality, volume and depth can leave you feeling a little breathy, so make sure you do breathing exercises before you speak.

Breathe from below your diaphragm (belly breathing) and practise a few good deep breaths beforehand. Be aware of your breathing and slow down if you find your voice getting higher or you are speaking quickly. This enables you to get more air.

So, we've prepared ourselves as best possible and are aware of the need to use our voice as an essential instrument. What else do we need to consider when wanting to add magic to our tales?

Use of Pauses and Silence

"It is in the space between the words where the real story is told."
Clare Edwards

Pauses and silence are two of the most powerful storytelling tools you have and, in my opinion, are grossly underutilised. If you watch the great orators of our time like Winston Churchill, Nelson Mandela, Dr Martin Luther King Jr., Barack Obama, Emma Watson, Malala Yousafzai and Oprah Winfrey, their use of silence can be deafening.

Let's have a look at how we can use pauses and silence for effect.

Attention - when we first go to tell our story, just to stand in front of our audience in a neutral position and stay silent will command their attention more than any noise or request you can make. It also signals to the audiences' brains to move into listening mode. For you as the storyteller, it gives you time to get your breathing right, think about what you are going to say and tune in to your audience.

Rapport – as well as speaking with your voice, every other part of your physiology and mind is able to connect with your audience. Take time to make eye contact with your listeners; for maximum connection let your eyes rest on individuals for about three seconds, no longer, no shorter, and remember to smile with your eyes.

Pacing – if we have done our job properly then we will have practised our story time and time again. We are therefore so familiar with it that we sometimes forget what the experience is like for our listeners, hearing it for the first time. Remember that as we are telling our story, our audience is creating its own representation, and our pausing allows them to catch up to and stay with us.

You can use pacing to build up and tease the audience. One of the key stories from my life is how I met my husband. First, I tell the story of how we met in England and then I share an epiphany I had whilst packing to come to Australia. I go on to link the two stories together with a powerful experience I had 6 months before I met Jason, and it is in the pacing that the power of the story and the message that I want to convey is suddenly understood in an 'aha' moment. (see my Little Learning Gem)

Humour – if there's one criticism I have of some speakers and storytellers that use humour, it's that they don't give their listeners enough time to get the joke! Our brains are still computing the double entendre, innuendo or subtle play on words and off races the speaker to the next piece of prose. Timing and humour are a skill, so practise lots and remember…………………… it's the pause that holds the punch.

Anticipation and Tension – pauses are powerful. As creatures of meaning, when we are listening to a story, we are trying to figure out and predict what happens next - whether consciously or subconsciously. Pausing adds to the 'what next' level of anticipation, where we are wondering if our guess was correct or not. Our story will contain natural pause breaks, so it's important to work out where they are and pause an extra second or two to let the audience either figure it out or find a new route if they were wrong.

Empathy – our story may be one of our life experiences and sometimes these can be difficult and challenging tales. Pausing as the storyteller will help you gather yourself together at that time where you need a little courage to continue, without going too deep into the emotion. It also gives the audience time to resonate with your story and come to grips with the fact that you are sharing something deep and vulnerable of yourself. If you want your audience to deeply connect with your story and build mutual empathy, then give them time to do so.

How long? - a word to the wise: avoid using pauses in the way that has become popular on contestant shows these days i.e. interminably long – it will irritate your audience and break rapport. Use pauses intelligently.

Use of Suspense and Surprise

We love surprises! We also love to listen to a story that builds suspense as we are busy trying to figure out the plot, the ending or the next turn. Many of the '101 Inspiring Stories for Business and Life' build as they develop or have a twist at the end. It never ceases to make me smile when I tell them and the response from the audience is palpable.

How can you add suspense to your story? Try to put yourself in your listener's shoes and anticipate a typical ending - then change it ONLY if the context is kept and fits with your message.

Use of Character in Story

Think about the stories you listened to as a child, or the stories you tell your children. The different characters were always an interesting, even exciting part of the story. We can still play characters as adults, even in business storytelling – it's all part of building interest and rapport with your audience.

A Sprinkling of Magic

It's important to do what you are comfortable with and to stay true to yourself. At the same time, if you can bring your characters to life, then you are adding another dimension of connection.

When I was young, we had a storytelling program in the UK called '*Jackanory*' and well-known actors used to read the books sitting in a chair. I was riveted every day from beginning to end as they changed their voices dramatically to represent each character. I'd often close my eyes and jump into the world of the story, and it was the storyteller's mastery of character voice that made it all the easier for me to escape and picture the characters in detail.

Acting your Character out - first get a visual image of your character as this will help you transition from being you to being them. Notice everything about them from how they look, sound, move and speak. What voice does the character have, is there an accent, is there a stutter or a lisp, are they breathy or booming?

How do they present themselves? For example, you might have a naturally strong and upright posture and people know you are going into character as you lower and round your shoulders, move your head in a different direction or stoop. Have fun with this and experiment.

If using character voices feels at all uncomfortable then don't do it – it's important that you can convey the message authentically and in your own unique way.

Audience Interaction

Having your audience take part in your story, whether from their chairs or with you on stage, is always a winner. Interaction is an important element of rapport building and will set both a comfort and confidence level from the outset. An exaggerated example of audience interaction in storytelling is Pantomime (you may want to look this up if you are not familiar with the term).

Use of Questions

You might want to pepper questions throughout your story to keep the audience involved. Make sure however that your questions only require a nod or an "aha" so that you retain control. Here are some suggestions:

Universal Truth - what we mean by this is a statement or rhetorical question that instantly connects you with your audience. If you are a manager sharing a story about yourself and it included for example something you failed at and learned from, you might want to open with a question like *"Would you agree that some of the most valuable lessons we can learn originate from some of our greatest stuff-ups?"*

The Power of Three - asking three simple questions before you start your storytelling is a highly effective way to gain inclusion from the audience as you anticipate three different responses. This also ensures full inclusion as you cater to differing styles

Try to make question 1 the question that your greatest advocates will want to say yes to, as this builds a positive energy and rapport.

For example:-

1. *"Who here loves a powerful and compelling story?"*

2. *"Who thought stories were confined to children at bedtime or gossip mongers?"*

3. *"And how many of you are simply curious as to how we could use stories to influence, inspire and make a difference?"*

My example above is about storytelling; however, your questions will be related to your topic.

Tag Questions (Question Tags) - this is a simple statement finished off with a question that elicits a nod either way, preferably in the affirmative. For example, *"We're all so busy these days; we're struggling to find time to take a breath and just enjoy doing nothing, aren't we?"* or

"Really learning to actively and openly listen to our staff and customers could make the difference between us being good and being exceptional, couldn't it?"

The tag is the *"aren't we?"* and *"couldn't it?"* but you can find any statement and finish it with an *"isn't it? won't you? will you? shall we? couldn't we?"* or similar question.

Peppered Questions - these are questions that are thrown in at a specific point in your story. You will already have experience of peppered questions in storytelling with children. These questions re-fire the neurology and bring us back into the story.

If your story builds up in suspense or has a twist to it, using peppered questions is a highly effective way to gee up the audience. For example, you can really play with this then stop at a crucial point, pause and ask the audience, with a wide grin, *"Who would like to know what happens next?"*

Take a Vote - you could, at a strategic point in your story, ask the audience either for their suggestions or give them a couple of options. For example, at a crucial point in your story you could ask:

"Who in all honesty, at this point, would have given up, walked away and heaved a sigh of relief?" then, *"And how many of you would have dug your heels in, persisted till the bitter end and regardless of the outcome?"* followed by *"So who would like to know what **I** decided to do?"*

Inoculation - this is similar to the Power of Three and is a way of proactively handling potential objections that you think might arise from or during your story. For example, you could open by acknowledging that when you told your story for the first time that there were three types of people in the audience – sceptical, cynical and ambivalent, yet when they decided to take those specific 'hats' off for the hour, a change in mindset occurred that they hadn't anticipated. This example also instils a sense of curiosity in your audience.

In short, anticipate and address potential objections upfront to build unconscious rapport (and proactively avoid potential sticky moments).

Questions I could use

Eye Contact

Making eye contact with your listeners is an essential element of building rapport. They say that the eyes are the windows to the soul and as such, when you connect through your eyes, you are building a relationship. How long you maintain eye contact for is also important; too short and there's no connection, too long and the listener may feel uncomfortable.

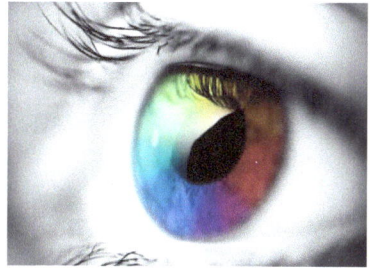

Let your eyes rest on the individual for about three seconds then gracefully move on. Avoid doing the overly obvious 'W' scans as it will look unnatural and forced.

Make sure that when you are making eye contact that your facial expression is non-threatening (unless it's at a part of the story that requires it and is therefore appropriate). You can also use your eyes to soften your glance and smile with your eyes. You will be amazed how many of your audience will mirror your look in response; it's like the storyteller's handshake or hug.

A Sprinkling of Magic

Facial Expressions

Some of us are more naturally expressive than others and the degree to which you use facial expressions in your storytelling is, of course, up to you. If you do feel comfortable however, then your expressions can add another dimension of life to your story.

People who are more introverted can struggle with deliberate or exaggerated facial expressions; extraverts find this much easier. If this is outside of your comfort zone, start small and practise in the mirror, recounting your story and considering where a small gesture might add authenticity, emphasis or drama. Be aware of how small hand gestures can bring your story even further to life.

Notice in as much detail as you can with each of the facial expressions and hand gestures below, what the message is they are conveying:

It may just be a crinkling of the eyes, a raising of the eyebrows, a look to the heavens or a mouth open wide, but our facial expressions can literally speak for themselves.

Facial expressions are as important as the words we use, particularly to visual learners, and bring our stories to life.

Deliberate Gestures – The Satir Categories

Building on the facial expressions, deliberate gestures can also become part of our story language. If you are delivering your story sitting down, then your facial expressions and hand gestures will be of greater importance. If you are standing and delivering your story, every gesture will form a part of your narrative, so really think about how you come across. You don't want to be wandering aimlessly through or making gestures that are inconsistent with the message in your story.

If you want to develop your stage presence and use of body language, then I suggest you sign up for a good public speaking course in your area (preferably on recommendation) and consider becoming a member of Toastmasters International or a Professional Speakers Association if there is one in your area.

Psychotherapist Virginia Satir (1916–1988) specialised in family therapy and was considered one of the most outstanding therapists in her time. Her work was studied by the co-founders of Neuro Linguistic Programming, John Grinder and Richard

A Sprinkling of Magic

Bandler, and from this came a series of personality types called the Satir Categories (also known as Satir Gestures).

Satir noticed that certain personality types used a pattern of gestures and it is these gestures that we will briefly cover. The personalities are more comprehensive and for the purpose of this guide I will focus only on the gestures.

Because I am using the Satir gestures as examples of effective body language, the descriptions I give do not necessarily relate to Satir's findings.

Study each of the poses below and think how you could implement them to some degree in your story to add emphasis and effectiveness to your message. I have used my own terminology with the official Satir terms in brackets:

The Pleaser (Placater) - this gesture gives the audience the message of wanting to please, to show slight submission or be non-confrontational. It's a way of saying:

- I'm sorry, forgive me
- Listen to me please
- Bear with me
- I stuffed up - sorry
- I'm looking for sympathy
- I want you to like me

To stay congruent with this pose you would most likely soften your voice, almost apologetically and tilt your head.

The Asserter (Leveller) - this is one of the most powerful or assertive gestures and says *"this is how it is"*. It can be used to convey difficult news without aggression or apology. It can also convey authenticity and honesty as in *"I'm levelling with you here"*.

In this image the hands are almost in a 'stop' gesture, facing downwards as if to say *"that's my message – take it or leave it"*. You can also make a levelling movement by sweeping your hands down and to the side.

It's an honest and fair gesture and gives the message of assertion and control.

The Pointer (Blamer) - this gesture is dominant and authoritarian. You may want to use it to strongly reinforce your message but be sure to use it sparingly as, if used out of context or frequently, you may break rapport with your audience. Examples of messages that this gesture reinforces either verbally or subconsciously include:

- DON'T make the same mistake as me
- NEVER lose sight of your goals
- This is the MOST important part of my message
- YOU and only YOU are responsible for your results

You will find your audience sits up, pays attention and takes notice if you use the pointer. If you want to make this gesture slightly less confronting, then point with all of your fingers in a semi-open hand gesture. You MUST be in rapport to use this gesture to effect.

The Reflector (Computer) - this pensive gesture is very powerful when you want your audience to be contemplative and reflective. They may subconsciously go into reflection mode themselves.

If you are taking questions from your audience and want time to reflect before answering, this is an ideal gesture to use and buy yourself time.

The reflector is also an effective gesture to use when you are talking to yourself, for example, *"And I thought to myself, how can I make this work, there must be a way?"* or *"And I asked myself, what can I learn from this experience that means that I won't ever make the same mistake again?"* It also invokes a sense of curiosity.

This stance can also give you an air of authority but unlike the pointer is non-threatening and can have a calming effect on your audience.

The Clown (Distracter) – there probably won't be too many occasions when you will want to use the clown! It does however grab your audience's attention. If you want to really lighten things up in your story and change the mood, then you could include the clown by means of waving your hands around or doing a silly dance.

I do the Bouncebackability dance in my Emotional Resilience Programs and it really lifts the mood. Professional speaker Amanda Gore uses the clown expertly in her keynote presentations to build rapport and to connect and relax her audience, making them more open to her message. It also helps them to get over any embarrassment as they participate.

A Sprinkling of Magic

A watered-down version of the clown is effective for bringing humour into your story or telling a joke. It can also help build rapport with your audience if you are traditionally known for being aloof or reserved (don't overdo it though, or they'll lock you up!).

Neutral Stance – Though not related to the Satir gestures, this is probably the position you most want to practise and use. When you are telling your story, you want the audience to connect with you and your content. If you keep wandering up and down the room or stage then your audience will lose interest and the message can be lost. They'll probably get dizzy too.

Neutral stance at first may feel awkward – where do I put my hands? After a while though it will feel natural and you will be more effective and expressive when your facial expressions and gestures are natural, deliberate and complement rather than detract from your story and message.

Avoid at all costs telling your story with a clicking pen in hand or both hands in your pockets and, even worse, jiggling coins! Your audience expects you to be confident, so gestures like this might well come across as more disrespectful than nervous.

Movement and Spontaneity

If your audience is relatively small or you are highly visible, you may want to use a chair to tell your story if you feel it will add to your listener's experience. Make sure that everyone can see you though and that you can still project your voice and breathe easily. This is equally true if you are telling your story from a wheelchair.

You can still move and gesture from a chair by using shoulder and arm movements and leaning in is particularly effective. Just as you are coming to a core message, pause, lean forwards and lower your voice. You now have your audience captured.

If you are going to move – move with volition. Don't stand there like you need to go to the toilet, shifting your weight from foot to foot – it makes the audience uncomfortable. Find your centre of balance and keep your weight equal on both feet. To find your centre of balance, imagine you have a piece of string tied to your navel and pulling down directly to the ground. Just stand for a few moments and you will find it as it will feel comfortable.

If you want to be truly spontaneous, you might want to choose a part of your story to come out into the audience and surprise them or move right to the front of the stage before you deliver your surprise.

A Sprinkling of Magic

Stage Anchoring

You may want to use the stage deliberately to 'anchor' certain elements of your story. What this means in simple terms is that you use the stage as a path for your journey and have the audience connect where you are standing with certain points of your story.

For example, if you are telling your story and it involves a negative emotion, you might want to find a specific spot on the stage just for this part of the story. As the story evolves, you can then take the audience with you metaphorically AND spatially. The NLP term for this is stage anchoring or spatial anchoring.

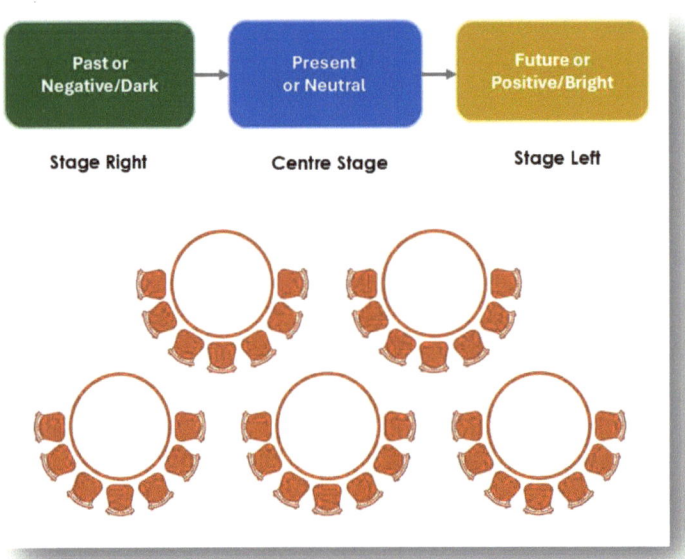

As you metaphorically leave the dark past behind, you can also do so physically as you move to the centre of the stage then over to the other side to talk about the brighter future.

Be aware of Lighting - if you are talking about a dark past, you don't want a super shiny spotlight on you. Likewise, if you are moving to a brighter future, make sure you are not in a blind spot where there is no or little light. Practise with this first because you want to be really comfortable with it. You don't want your story to lose its impact because you've been worrying about where you should be standing. Remember - **If in doubt, leave it out.**

Tense - Past or Present?

Whether you want to be a present or past tense raconteur depends on a few considerations. If you want to change the pace of the story and add effect, it can be a good idea to switch from past to present tense. You can narrate the outline and the lead up in past tense then, for effect, bring everyone with you 'in the moment'.

A Sprinkling of Magic

For example (this is a true story from my days in the hospitality industry):

> *"So there I am, wearing nothing but a pair of old odd socks and I open the door ever so slightly to put on the 'Do not Disturb' sign. As I try to pop the sign over the doorknob, it flutters to the floor so I bend down to pick it up and ... click ... the door automatically shuts behind me. Dear God, what to do now?*
>
> *I suddenly spy a rather attractive Yucca plant next to the lift and have to make two immediate and important calculations: 1. Will I make it in time? and 2. Are the leaves wide enough to cover my modesty?"*

If you are sharing a story from your experience that is of a sensitive or emotional nature, then I would recommend you keep it in past tense as this allows you an element of distance and an ability to remain disassociated from the emotion.

Person - First or Third?

If you are telling your story and it is of a sensitive nature, in addition to using tense to help you dissociate and remain in control of your emotions, you might want to practise by recounting it in the 3rd person; either for the whole of the story if you don't want your audience to identify you directly as the main character, or for the majority of the story then switching to first person.

I encourage you to check out video footage of Dr Janet Lapp (better still – try and get to see her on stage) who tells her very emotional story exquisitely and changes from third to first person at a crucial point. This is truly a skill of a master storyteller and will hold your audience's attention unquestionably.

I'm Just like You

A powerful way to build rapport with your audience is to have them feeling that you're just like them. This is particularly important when the story you are telling is your own. Show people that you are as human and vulnerable as they are and they will instantly build a bridge of trust with you, provided of course it is authentic.

Examples of simple and slightly humorous *"I'm just like you"* phrases include:

- *If I had a dollar for every time I've made this mistake, I'd be telling you this story from my private jet*
- *I never for one moment thought I'd be standing here in front of you today with my story ...*
- *I was so scared of public speaking I couldn't even announce the raffle at the local social club!*

- *I'd never considered using stories to get my message across; I thought they were for children. (Then I read a great book called 'A Sprinkling of Magic'!)*
- *For so long I just couldn't see the light at the end of the tunnel, I thought I'd be in this mess forever, then …*

Little Learning Gems

I have listened to hundreds of speakers' stories and one of the benchmarks I use to differentiate between a good story and a magical one is how the storyteller uses what I call 'Little Learning Gems' or 'LLG's'. These are phrases or revelations that become turning points; they're the expressions speakers use to bring the story together, let it unfold, provide the solution or key understandings, and generally connect with the audience in a special way.

Little Learning Gems need to be delivered in a way that the message is precious and needs to be handled with deliberation and care. Let it unfold slowly, making sure to hold eye contact with your audience, letting them know that this is a really important part of the story. Pause before you reveal your Little Learning Gem. Let me share with you a couple of LLG's that I use:

In one of my personal stories, I recount something that happened when I was packing to come and live in Australia with my Mr Right. I'm sitting on the floor of my dining room, drowning in papers, files, photos and books and I spot a laminated piece of paper that I faintly recognise. As I gently squeeze it out from the bottom of the pile, my ear to ear grin kicks off a rising warmth of love and laughter simultaneously. I read the words and shake my head, nodding in violent agreement with every stage.

[Enter Little Learning Gem] It is at this point that I realise that the intention I set at a workshop two years and two months earlier, on 20 February 2002 at two minutes past eight (the date being 200220022002), had materialised. Every milestone I had identified had come true and, not only had it come true, it had materialised within days or weeks of when I said it would.

My self-fulfilling prophecy had come to fruition, and for the first time in my life it was a good one; one that I had yearned for all my life.

When I tell my 'Donkey in the Well' story, I pause at the end of the story and pick up a stone. I then look at my audience and say slowly, deliberately and with volition:

"It was the self-same stones that were the donkey's potential death knell that, after a moment's realisation and inspiration, became its saving grace. What are some of the potential gifts in your life that you have been encountering that have been presenting as obstacles or challenges?"

Use of Reverse Psychology

If you sense that you risk coming across as condescending in your story with the meaning you want to convey, consider using reverse psychology. This is where you deliberately advocate the opposite of the message you are wanting to get across, so that it provokes a reaction in your audience to the opposite effect i.e. they end up agreeing with your real message.

Let's take the example of when I was the Hotel Memo Queen, when I tell my story about my lack of awareness of my management style. I could say the following in the context of effective communication:-

"I'm sure you would all agree that writing and sending numerous dictatorial memos, despite the fact that there were weekly team meetings and daily handovers, is a highly effective way to communicate in a motivational and inspiring manner!" This then opens the debate for the audience to input their ideas on what IS a motivational form of effective team communication.

One form of reverse psychology that Dr Janet Lapp uses to great effect, is where she 'assumes' the audience is already expertly using the strategies she is suggesting. She will show us a highly effective strategy then throw in, almost as an add-on, that we are of course already using this strategy….aren't we? She uses all the Secret Magic Ingredients to deliver this in a way that keeps her audience 'on her side' and at the same time provokes us to realise that we need to adopt the strategies she is suggesting.

Planned Spontaneity

Yes, it sounds like an oxymoron but planned spontaneity can be extremely effective when storytelling. Some ideas for creating spontaneity include:

- Joining your audience (if you are on stage) for a particular element of the story. Make sure though that your voice amplification is still of good quality and you can still be seen by everyone

- Using technology to add a surprise element e.g. have a voice recording that booms out from nowhere when you say *"and he said to me"*... Be prepared for hiccups with technology though

- Having your audience become part of your story. This is where you can introduce props (see next chapter for more ideas) and have audience members become the characters. This is effective in business storytelling where you want the team members to create the ending to the story

- Use symbols and props to identify characters. These can include:
    - Badges, hats, signs (hold them or place around your neck)

A Sprinkling of Magic

- A magic wand – you can ask your audience volunteer (or a team member) to wave their magic wand and share what would be different about the situation/scenario/story
- Puppets to represent the characters

In Summary

Take an inventory of what you already do or are naturally good at doing, then gradually add on elements and practise with them. Not all my suggestions will suit you – you may need to try a few jackets on first before you find those that comfortably fit. Remember also to take into account what your audience will interpret or perceive as 'magic ingredients'.

The masterful storyteller makes everything look so easy, and it is precisely because they have invested time and energy in the little things that will make the biggest difference. Every hand gesture, every pause, every facial expression will have been consciously rehearsed until they have climbed the ladder of learning and become unconsciously competent.

Still there they won't rest as they find increasingly more magic ingredients to captivate their audience.

Thoughts and Ideas from Secret Magic Ingredients

Chapter Eleven

The use of Props and Symbols

A Sprinkling of Magic

CHAPTER 11. THE USE OF PROPS AND SYMBOLS

In this section, I share with you examples of how speakers and storytellers use their props and symbols. Please respect their unique ownership and exclusive right to use – thank you.

A prop is effectively a symbol or physical metaphor for your message and should positively enhance your audience's experience and aim to help them assimilate the message at a deeper level.

Not everyone loves using props. Regardless of your opinion, props used well can add another dimension to your storytelling and are particularly memorable for highly visual learners.

In my brain-based keynotes I bring 'Brian the Brain' out. My brain comes in two halves and it's then easy for me to open it up and explain relevant neuroscience simply.

In my workshops I often set the scene using a 'magic wand'. It's a humorous way to let people know that there is no silver bullet, no magic wand, no 'fast track' (note the power of 3 there), and that they have to put the work in themselves once they have learned the strategies.

Two professional speakers I have seen use props and symbols with effortless ease are Peter Merrett and Tim Gard. Peter shares his story of training as a chef and will often wheel out a chopping board with lemons, cutting them as he shares his story. Tim reveals his hilarious 'official policy manual', suitcase and a multitude of props. Study footage of these speakers, how they use their props, how they bring them into their story and enhance the whole experience for the audience.

Props as Gifts, Giveaways or Product

When I last saw Tim speak, his presentation used the metaphor of 'losing my marbles'. As we left the auditorium, we were each presented with a little bag of six coloured marbles with a little card inside, all in a black velour bag. Do you think this helps us remember Tim's message more effectively? You bet!

When I tell my 'Donkey in the Well' story, I interpret it and use the stones as a metaphor for the gift in the challenge. After delivering my little learning gem I then bring out my treasure chest which contains flat round-coloured pebbles and some permanent markers.

Once everyone has a pebble in their hands, I ask them to write down the gift on their pebble and keep it as a reminder that there is always a gift to be found in the challenge, even if we might not be aware of it until much later down the track.

A Sprinkling of Magic

The pebbles cost me just a few dollars per pack, yet their ripple effect is priceless. If you haven't got money for having props professionally made, don't worry – use your imagination.

'Gingernuts at the Airport' is one of my favourite metaphors for the consequences of making assumptions. I use this story often when running workshops on excellence in communication and active listening skills.

When people come into the workshop, I usually have a plate of gingernuts on the table and participants just see them as an offering with morning or afternoon tea.

As I tell the story and am coming to the end, I give every participant a packet of gingernuts and leave them with the thought, *"Next time you go to jump to a conclusion or make a hasty assumption, CHECK YOUR GINGERNUTS!"*

Stimulus and Response

By using props in this way we are helping people make a concrete connection between our message and the prop. The next time they see a packet of gingernut biscuits or a coloured pebble, what do you think will pop into their mind? In NLP we call this subtle influencing 'anchoring'. It is happening all the time and all around us.

Think about your favourite song, it will most likely be linked with an experience and immediately you are taken back to the time when you first heard the song, or the song was linked to the experience.

To use your props and symbols to their greatest effect, keep them out of sight until you need them, then reveal them in a way that the audience feels like they are being let into a special secret.

In one of my keynotes, I share a very personal story called 'My String of Pearls' that involves a past history of domestic violence, and I use the metaphor of how a pearl forms, to talk about the layering of resilience. At the very end of my story, I reach into a beautiful red and gold velvet pouch and put the pearl necklace around my neck. It's one of the most powerful demonstrations of props I have ever used.

In Summary

Props and symbols used with volition and as an enhancer to an already strong story can transform your story from good to great AND make it more memorable. Practise until you feel comfortable and, if possible, trademark your props and symbols for your unique and exclusive use.

Props and symbols have the power to differentiate you as a speaker and can be the greatest contributors to your uniqueness. They are a special rapport building secret magic ingredient!

Ideas, Thoughts and Notes

Chapter Twelve

How to Construct your Story
A Seven Step Process

CHAPTER 12. HOW TO CONSTRUCT YOUR STORY - A SEVEN STEP PROCESS

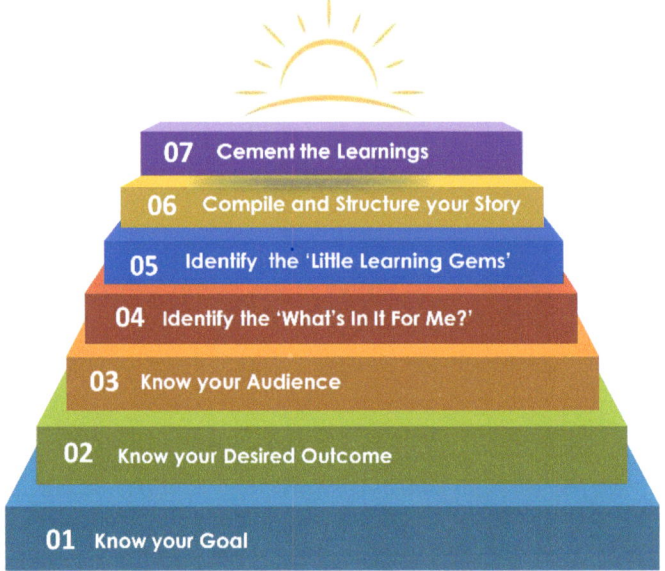

Now folks – this isn't rocket science. It's very simple really; your story needs to have a beginning, a middle and an end. I know this is stating the 'blooming obvious' but is still needs to be said – we want a story, not a lot of waffle.

Before you even put pen to paper or hit the keyboard, there are a number of points to consider that will ensure your story hits home with its message and the meaning.

Step 1 – Know your Goal

- What's your WHY? What is the purpose of telling your story?
- What is the message you want to convey or the lesson to be learned?
- Why is this story important? Why does it need to be shared?

We are now building on everything that has gone before and constructing our story using all the parameters from the previous chapters.

My Goal

A Sprinkling of Magic

Step 2 – Know your Desired Outcome

- What do you want your audience to be experiencing once you have told your story? How do you want them to react?
- What state of mind do you want to leave your audience in? For example, do you want them to be:
    - In a reflective state
    - Full of questions and curiosity
    - Engaging in active dialogue with each other and you
    - Inspired to action
    - Questioning their existing ways and considering the possibility of alternatives
    - Increasing their attitude to risk
    - Processing and reaching an 'aha' moment
    - Wanting to do even better

NB. I would strongly advise against an outcome that leaves someone with a negative emotion e.g. feeling guilty or ashamed.

My Desired Outcome

```
┌─────────────────────────────────────────────────────────────────────────┐
│                                                                         │
│                                                                         │
│                                                                         │
│                                                                         │
│                                                                         │
│                                                                         │
└─────────────────────────────────────────────────────────────────────────┘
```

Step 3 – Know your Audience

- What's the profile of your audience? What are they likely to be interested in so that you can adapt your story to their interests?
- Are the majority of the audience members likely to be more rational or creative, literal or inferential listeners, dreamers or pragmatists? This is essential to the language you will use in your story – too analytical and the emotional listeners turn off, too emotional and the analytical listeners won't buy into it.

My Audience Profile

```
┌─────────────────────────────────────────────────────────┐
│                                                         │
│                                                         │
│                                                         │
│                                                         │
└─────────────────────────────────────────────────────────┘
```

Step 4 – Identify the WIIFM (what's in it for me?) for your Listener

- Why would this story interest the listener?
- How can your offerings enrich their experience?
- What can you find out about your audience in advance?
- How specifically will they benefit from hearing your message?
- How can you customise your story to make it unique to them?
- How can you create the story in a way that will hold the listener's attention?

Key Benefits

```
┌─────────────────────────────────────────────────────────┐
│                                                         │
│                                                         │
│                                                         │
│                                                         │
└─────────────────────────────────────────────────────────┘
```

Step 5 – Identify the Little Learning Gems

- What are the most memorable, most effective and most impactful points of your story?
- What can't be left out, even if you had to cull 50%?
- What is the story's 'crescendo'?
- Where are you going to place your significant pauses?
- How might you want to create suspense and excitement?
- What are the Little Learning Gems in terms of 'aha' moments?

A Sprinkling of Magic

Learning Gems and Essentials

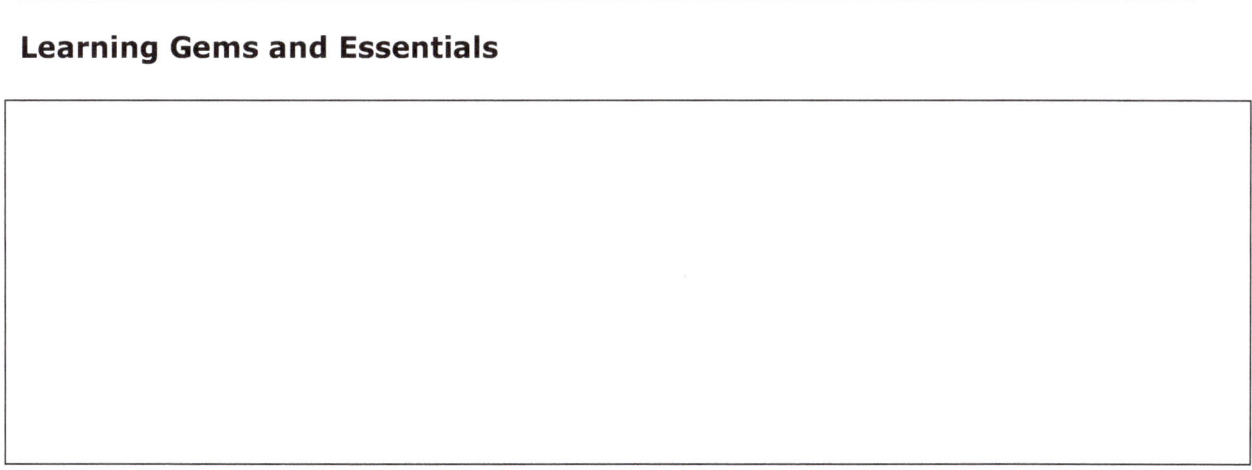

Step 6 – Compile and Structure your Story

So now you want to bring it all together and write it. Remember, whether it's a business-related story, a parable or an extended metaphor, you want to take your audience on a journey.

Set the Scene – this is an essential element of preparing your audience and shouldn't be skimped on. You are preparing your audience to be receptive to your message. You may want to add some more detail to the background, but not so much that the WHY people are wondering what's the point, your WHAT people are confused and your HOW people are doodling! (see Learning Styles). Be clear, concise and confident.

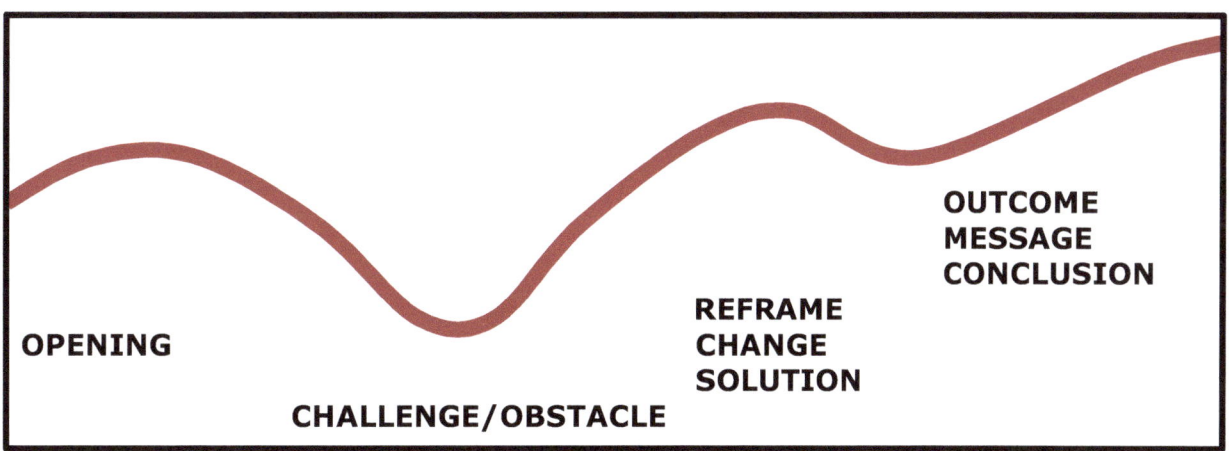

Opening - make sure that your opening captures the attention of your audience. You may even want to ask their permission to tell the story. Just a simple, *"Do you mind if I share a short story with you?"* and you will know if this is appropriate or relevant for your situation.

Sometimes you want your audience to realise that you are about to tell a story and sometimes it may be more effective to drop into it conversationally. Ways to start your story in this manner can include:

A Sprinkling of Magic

- *That reminds me of a time when …*
- *And when I thought of this a little story came to mind …*
- *And it got me thinking about …*
- *Do you remember when? …*
- *What if I told you? …*
- *It was the morning of [date] and there I was …*
- *I remember my grandfather sitting me down and saying...*
- *There's a story related to this that I've never forgotten …*
- *Something in the news caught my eye today and triggered my memory of …*
- *Do you mind if I sit down, there's something I'd like to share with you...*
- *Would you mind if I share an experience I once had?*
- *Whenever I think of X, a story I've never forgotten comes to mind*
- *Who would have thought, but this actually happened to me...*

You can also open your story with a question relating to the content or nature of the story you are about to tell. The more imaginatively you build it, the deeper they'll engage.

As an opening to my (now very well-heeled!) 'Donkey in the Well' story, I usually ask if any of the audience members have ever been to any of the Southern Mediterranean countries like Greece, Spain or Portugal. I then ask them if they've ever seen the poor donkeys that are so overladen it looks like they could do the splits at any moment. Then I begin to tell them about a time when I was on holiday in a little town in the foothills of Southern Spain and there was a real commotion around one of the farmers and his old donkey …

My Opening

A Sprinkling of Magic

Outline the Challenge or Obstacle - if your story includes challenges, personal pain or difficult issues, make sure you don't keep the audience there too long as what might happen is that they empathise with you and go into your pain (or their own pain) or they become detached and close down.

Consider also the amount of detail you want to go into; what is enough to get your point across, because you don't want people to recoil from you. It might be that a bit of calibration is needed and I would advise that you run the story past a few people you know well first.

Neither do you want to trivialise your challenge if this is the major point of the story. Make sure your body language and voice delivery are congruent with your message and you will know from the reaction of your audience the degree to which your message is being understood or accepted.

My Challenge or Obstacle

Reframing – if your listeners are in one frame of mind and you want to move them to a different frame of mind, maybe one where they can see a solution, alternative or improvement, your aim is to help them to see things through a different 'frame' hence the term 'reframe'. The ability to change frames quickly after you have taken your audience through a challenging experience is essential. You must however stay authentic and make the transition smooth so as to maintain credibility.

When I tell one of my stories about my challenge to have children and our unsuccessful IVF attempts, I quickly move on to share with the audience how I believe it was a blessing in disguise and talk about my new goal of having 20 sponsored children all around the world. This immediately lifts the spirits of my audience and, of course, those who have been through a similar challenge, now have an alternative outcome to consider for themselves.

What can you use as part of reframing from your Secret Magic Ingredients, as a way to bring your audience back up in mood (e.g. change in tone, pace, speed, volume, facial expression, gestures, position)?

A Sprinkling of Magic

Reframing Ideas

```
[                                                                    ]
```

Outcome/Message/Conclusion – you may want to share your lessons with the audience or leave them to come to their own conclusions. You may want to throw a rhetorical question out to your audience or ask them why they thought you wanted to tell this particular story.

> If you want to leave your audience in a reflective state, be aware of the energy in the room and consider the impact this may have. In my experience, it is more effective to bring them back up again, even if it's by a small increment, rather than have them leave 'flat'.

You could facilitate a discussion around the story and have the audience come up with ideas, their unique interpretations, alternative outcomes, etc. An effective way to conclude is to make a connection to the beginning of your story, coming full circle so to speak and closing the story loop.

Ending – It's vital that your audience knows when you have come to the end of your story. I have seen too many speakers end up in an uncomfortable sticky situation when the audience is still quiet and waiting for the last 'chunk'. Make sure your voice is strong, clear and you acknowledge the ending in some way with your physiology (e.g. a bow, a wink, a smile, a hand clasp, hands down on the table or open to the audience).

My Conclusion and Ending

```
[                                                                    ]
```

A Sprinkling of Magic

Secret Magic Ingredients and Props Reminder - which of the secret ingredients will add the most magic to your story? Which of the elements of captivation do you want to continue to develop and practise? Revisit your ideas captured at the end of Chapter 10.

If you are going to use props or symbols, where in your story will you use them? How will you use them, what will you use and why are you using them? Remember to eat the elephant one bite at a time and don't try and go from zero to hero in one fell swoop.

Step 7 – Cement the Learnings

How do you plan to cement the learnings? Will you hand out a gift at the end of your story or will you open up a discussion about the future? There are many ways to 'anchor' the meaning in your message, from subtle to obvious. It's a small but vitally important link for you to consider.

An effective way to cement learning is to have your audience create the follow through, the moral of the story or alternative endings; this gives them direct input and involvement and increases the likelihood that they will take action on your message.

Ideas for Cementing the Learnings

Example - Simple Story with Structure

Let's use a simple example of story structure from one of the 101 Inspiring Stories and Metaphors for Business and Life. This is a true story.

Starting Over

Opening and Scene Setting

It was a cold December night in West Orange, New Jersey. Thomas Edison's factory was humming with activity. Work was proceeding on a variety of fronts as the great inventor was trying to turn more of his dreams into practical realities. Edison's plant, made of concrete and steel, was deemed 'fireproof'. As you may have already guessed, it wasn't!

Challenge

On that frigid night in 1914, the sky was lit up by a sensational blaze that had burst through the plant roof. Edison's 24-year-old son, Charles, made a frenzied search for his famous inventor-father. When he finally found him, he was watching the fire. His white hair was blowing in the wind. His face was illuminated by the leaping flames. "My heart ached for him," said Charles. "Here he was, 67 years old, and everything he had worked for was going up in flames."

Reframe

When he saw me, he shouted, "Charles! Where's your mother?" When I told him I didn't know, he said, "Find her! Bring her here! She'll never see anything like this as long as she lives!"

Next morning, Thomas Edison looked at the ruins of his factory and said this of his loss: "There's value in disaster. All our mistakes are burned up. Thank God, we can start anew."

Outcome/Message/Conclusion

[You may want to leave this open ended and elicit from your audience why you decided to tell this particular story. Here is the message that usually accompanies this story]:

What a wonderful perspective on things that seem at first to be so disastrous. A business failure, divorce, personal dream gone sour ... whether these things destroy an individual depends largely on the attitude he or she takes toward them. Sort out why it happened and learn something from the blunders. Think of different approaches that can be taken.

Start over.

Not all stories of course will follow this structure, however the point is that your story should have a structure as this ensures that all the salient points are included and helps you to remember the story too. Re-read the story without looking for structure – can you feel yourself being taken on a journey?

Now complete a rough outline of your story, being consciously aware of the seven steps. Don't try to edit as you go along, just start writing. There is a space for you to do this but you might just want to get a piece of paper and start jotting ideas down. Try not to go directly digital as this really engages the logical parts of your brain and we want to keep stimulating the creative parts. You can also jot your ideas on

A Sprinkling of Magic

post-it notes and lay them out on a large piece of paper and move them around to develop your structure.

There's no right and wrong – just start! There's more room at the back of the book too.

In Summary

Master storytellers make it seem so easy. The story just rolls off their tongue and it doesn't seem like there was so much effort put in to constructing their story. But this is the way of the masters; they make it look easy.

Constructing your story will help you to deliver it in a professional and easy-going manner because you will have become so familiar with it through the construction process, that you will be at least consciously competent and well on the way to being unconsciously competent.

Practice makes perfect and the only way to fail is not to try at all!

My Story Outline

Chapter Thirteen

Positioning your Story

Chapter 13. Positioning your Story

There's really no hard and fast rule as to when and where you include your stories if you are using them as part of a speech, presentation or workshop. The main point is that your stories are used to illustrate a point and that the listener can find meaning in their message.

If you open up with a story immediately, make sure it's not too long (remember our practical preference logical listeners) or you could lose the audience quite quickly. Below are some suggestions based on what has worked well for me in the past (and still does) and are guidelines only:

To Set the Scene

Set the scene with something short, punchy and to the point. Delivered with volition and authenticity, an opening story can have your audience captivated from the get-go. If you really want to make a point, your opening story can demonstrate that you mean business; it's time to sit up and listen.

A story I sometimes use right at the beginning when I am running a teambuilding experience, and I know that there are some cynics in the audience, is the 'Three Hairs Metaphor' (which you can find in the 101 Inspiring Stories and Metaphors for Business and Life). This little story is all about attitude, is non-threatening and immediately gets to the point. I finish the story by saying *"And may you **choose** to have an exceptional day!"*

Scene Setting Ideas

```
┌─────────────────────────────────────────────────────────┐
│                                                         │
│                                                         │
│                                                         │
│                                                         │
│                                                         │
└─────────────────────────────────────────────────────────┘
```

As an Opening Metaphor

You may want to jump into a story soon after you have set the scene as a way to engage your audience to listen and help set the tone for the rest of your session. Keep it as a mood setting story or short, sharp and to-the-point so that the audience knows exactly what your overall theme and message is going to be. In my experience, long stories within the first 10 minutes can be a challenge to hold your audience's attention.

A Sprinkling of Magic

Opening Metaphor Ideas

```
┌─────────────────────────────────────────────────────────────┐
│                                                             │
│                                                             │
│                                                             │
│                                                             │
│                                                             │
└─────────────────────────────────────────────────────────────┘
```

As a Pace Changer

Somewhere in the middle of your session you can drop a story in to highlight a series of points you have been making or to take the session along a different track and lead into a new set of points. Remember to include your Secret Magic Ingredients to help make the transition clear.

You can also use a story at this stage to take your audience on a journey of digression and return to close it later, leaving them in a state of open curiosity (called open loop metaphor or nesting).

Pace Changing Ideas

```
┌─────────────────────────────────────────────────────────────┐
│                                                             │
│                                                             │
│                                                             │
│                                                             │
│                                                             │
└─────────────────────────────────────────────────────────────┘
```

As the Body

Your personal story (i.e. a story about yourself) is often best served as the meat in the sandwich so that your audience is in a highly receptive and active listening state; you have set the scene and now it's the ripe and right time to share your wisdom, knowledge and experience.

As a Closing Metaphor

Stories as a closer can be exceptionally powerful. They bring together all the key points you have been making and serve them up, as a finale, like a delicious dessert.

This is one time when you really don't want to add to the story in terms of asking the audience for input or offering a final point, moral or interpretation. The story can speak for itself, so make sure it's clear – to keep to our dessert analogy - not a serving of ice cream and cheese on the same plate! Make sure it's not too heavy and stodgy so people fall asleep with a spoon in their hands. And finally, make sure it's not too cryptic like the over-decorated desserts served up in fine dining restaurants with especially confusing cutlery!

Closing Metaphor Ideas

In Summary

Every time you want to tell a story, regardless of where you position it, make sure that it links directly with a point you want to make. Random stories don't cut it and will leave your audience confused or even bored.

Be aware however of not over-using stories as they can easily lose their meaning. I trained with an exceptionally gifted facilitator who, on one occasion, told five metaphorical stories in a row and lost his audience completely.

It is far better to weave your stories, to use them to enhance your message and to honour them as respected gifts.

Chapter Fourteen

How to remember Stories

A Sprinkling of Magic

CHAPTER 14. HOW TO REMEMBER STORIES

Because we all have differing learning preferences, there isn't going to be one correct way to remember stories. It really does depend on what will stick in our unique brains. Below are three processes I have used and am familiar with – choose which one appeals to you the most.

It goes without saying that the more familiar we are with our story, the more confident we will present it and the more we will feel comfortable enough to adlib or be spontaneous (planned or otherwise).

Repetition

The stories we were told as children can be easily remembered primarily because of repetition. We never tired of hearing our favourite story over and over and over again. This is a simple yet effective way of remembering a story, particularly if you have a structured, step by step, methodical learning preference.

Read your story a number of times the whole way through then break it down into bite size chunks and read and repeat, read and repeat, etc. Notice how you are recalling your story - can you 'see' the story written down and are you accessing it visually or can you hear yourself recounting the story in your own voice?

Pictures

If you find it easy to visualise, then sketch your story out in pictures. I use a simple clock system as you will see. Now I warn you, I'm no Picasso, but I'm happy to share my system with you. Let's take a simple story, The Boulder and the King.

In ancient times, a King had a boulder placed on a roadway. Then he hid himself and watched to see if anyone would remove the huge rock. Some of the king's wealthiest merchants and courtiers came by and simply walked around it. Many loudly blamed the King for not keeping the roads clear, but none did anything about getting the stone out of the way.

Then a farmer came along carrying a load of vegetables. Upon approaching the boulder, the farmer laid down his burden and tried to move the stone to the side of the road. After much pushing and straining, he finally succeeded.

After the farmer picked up his load of vegetables, he noticed a purse lying in the road where the boulder had been. The purse contained many gold coins and a note from the King indicating that the gold was for the person who removed the boulder from the roadway. The farmer learned what many of us never understand!

Every obstacle presents an opportunity to improve our condition.

OK – so here's my pictorial representation of the story ☺

I'm sure every single one of you can do better than me!

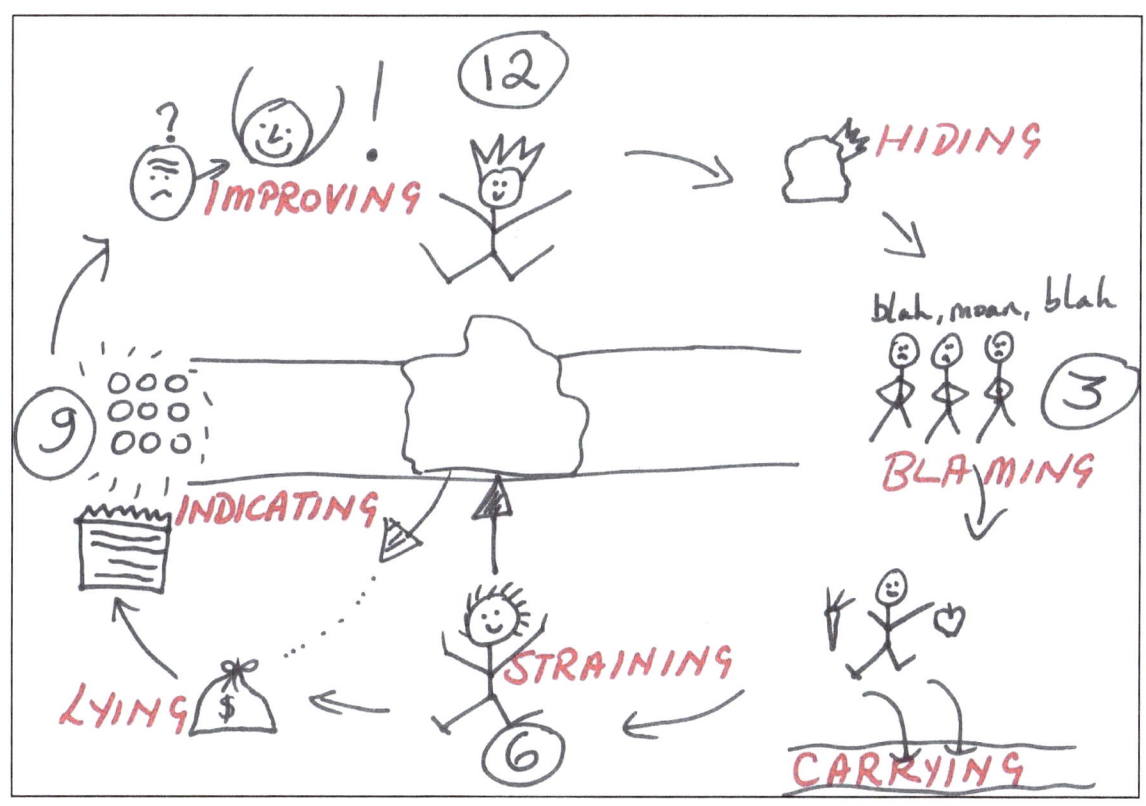

A Sprinkling of Magic

Using the Clock Numbers

It might not always pan out this way but when it does you can marry the images, linking words and clock numbers so that you really are using all parts of your brain to connect the story and remember it. This also helps you remember the correct sequence.

- ✓ The King had 12 jewels in his crown
- ✓ There were 3 courtiers blaming the king for the state of the road
- ✓ The farmer made 6 attempts to move the boulder
- ✓ There were 9 gold coins in the purse

Link'ING' Words

We can piece our story together by remembering certain words that are important linking elements of the story. It helps to keep them in present tense and research has proven that we remember 'ing' words (a gerund) more easily. So, look again at the 2nd drawing with the linking words I have chosen. These are the words you want to embed into your subconscious so that you become unconsciously competent.

Playback

Read the story out loud - slowly, clearly and audibly - and record it on your phone or other recording device so you can play it to yourself at leisure. Without the visuals i.e. just listening, you can really pick up those nuances of cadence, timbre, tone, pace and volume. Keep adjusting till you're 99% happy (we're never perfect!).

Story Sketching

I have mentioned many times in this workbook the benefits of keeping a notebook on you. Whenever a story comes to mind or you hear a story that appeals to you, have a go at sketching it out and adding the linking words. Read it through a couple of times then see how you go just recounting it from your sketch.

Like any exercise involving memory, practice makes perfect – you just have to start.

In Summary

Remembering stories becomes easier over time and finding different ways to engage your brain and memory can only increase your chances of recall. The more comfortable we become, the easier it is for the parts of our brain doing the recalling. If you are nervous about remembering a story, you could always set things up as if you were deliberately reading from a book; in which case I would buy an ornate old and very large book and hide your story in there, making it part of the experience!

My Story in a Nutshell

As I write this final section of my book, I am looking outside my office window at two large white sulphur crested cockatoos bullying a handful of rainbow lorikeets, and listening to the newly hatched clutch of four noisy miner birds in a nearby tree. I feel truly blessed with my story so far …

I grew up in the city of Liverpool, UK, the youngest of five. My life's dream was to be a ballerina but that was short lived – about as short as I turned out to be which is 4 feet 10 and three quarters or 1 metre 47centimetres!

Unsure of what career direction to take, I followed two of my elder siblings into the hospitality industry where I worked in the front of house section with various hotel chains.

Working in hospitality took me to jobs in The Netherlands and Switzerland and left me with lifelong friends. After nine happy and hard-working years in hotels, it was my dogged determination to become fluent in Dutch that became my passport to the corporate world where I worked for 13 years as a manager in Publishing and Information Technology.

The internet boom and bust year of 2001 led me to reconsider my vocation in life and I transitioned into people development, working for two of the UK's most prominent team development companies. My corporate career, though very successful, left me little time to find that special person in my life and it was in 2002 that I met my Mr Right at a music festival in the UK. He turned out to be Australian, thus began the next adventure!

In 2004 I left the UK to settle in Australia, on the stunningly beautiful Sunshine Coast of Queensland where I set up my business. Jason (Mr Right) and I made several attempts to expand our little family of two, but it wasn't to be, hence my goal to have a global family of 20 sponsored children.

Like many others, I have had my share of challenges; an abusive relationship in my teens, the mental scars of which I carried for too long; the death of both parents and our struggle to have children. I have used these challenges and how I learned to bounce back to develop my workshops on emotional resilience and thriving in change.

My story continues; each night before I go to sleep, I count my blessings and look forward to each new page and every exciting chapter. I have no idea what the future chapters hold, yet I will continue to embrace the uncertainty with excitement.

A SPRINKLING OF MAGIC – YOUR FEEDBACK IS APPRECIATED

My intention for this workbook is to provide you with the confidence, knowledge, tools and information to go out and use stories effectively in both business and life. The degree to which I have succeeded in my intention lies in your responses. I am keen to find out what value you have derived from the guide, how practical and informative you found it, was it useful and easy to follow? What, if anything would you want to add or change?

If you are interested in having me facilitate a storytelling workshop, please get in touch.

If 'A Sprinkling of Magic' has helped you in any way, I would value and appreciate your feedback in the form of a testimonial, no matter how short. If your feedback is of a constructive nature, then I would appreciate that too – you may even want to wrap it up in a story!

When I'm not writing books about storytelling I'm working with businesses as a Facilitator, Speaker and Coach. If you are interested in developing your people, then visit my BrainSmart People Development website www.brain-smart.com

clare@brain-smart.com

Tel :: (AU) +61 408 736 994
Tel :: (UK) +44 7713 499 350

101 Inspiring Stories and Metaphors for Business and Life

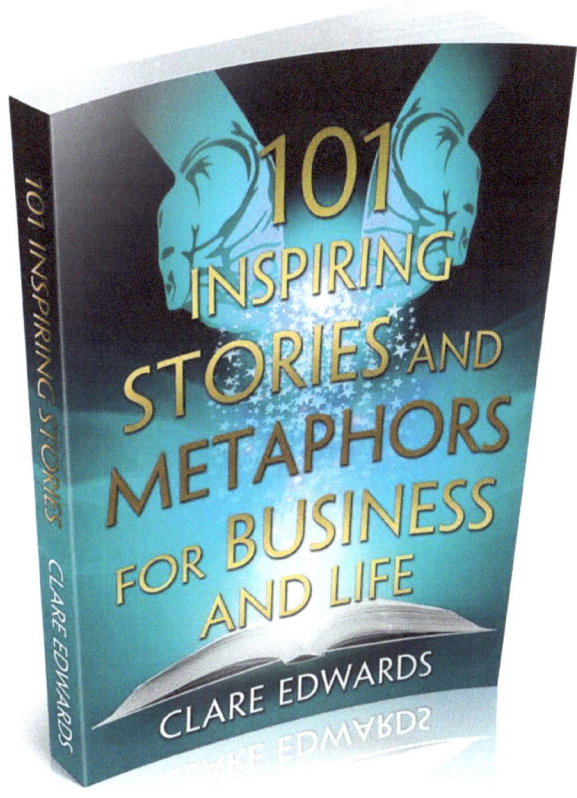

Where 'A Sprinkling of Magic' has taken you through the steps of constructing and delivering your stories for maximum effect, the aim of this e-book is to provide you with a rich and varied database of stories, some well-known and others lesser known, that have been categorised according to differing messages and meanings. These categories are ones that I have found to be useful and you may find a much wider application as you use them, so they shouldn't be restricted to the ones I suggest. Category examples include leadership, resilience, changing perspectives, values and accountability.

In addition to the categories, I have sometimes added my own notes, based on my experience of having told a particular story. This is designed to enhance the context for you in using the story and it is not my intention to provide you with an interpretation, as that of course, is down to you and your listener!

May you find an appropriate story for every message you wish to deliver, enjoy telling them, and always with A Sprinkling of Magic!

101 Inspiring Quotes for Business and Life

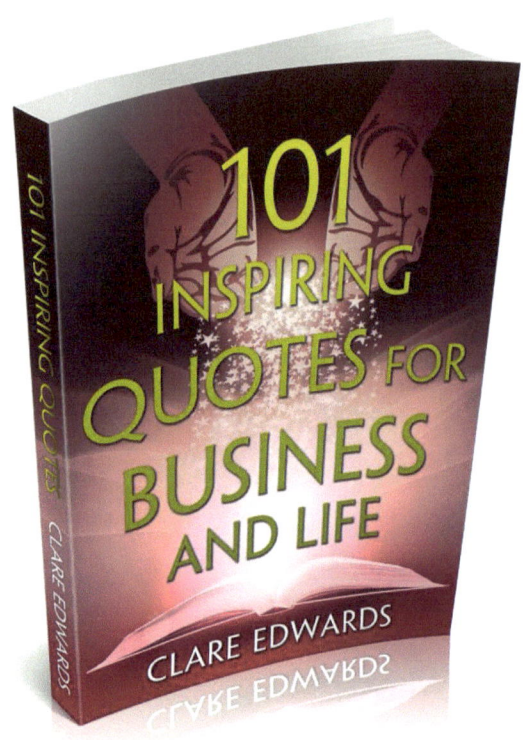

A quotation is like a mini power-packed story. It can be the magic ingredient in the recipe that brings out all the flavours of the metaphorical dish. If you want to credibly support your theory, then to do so with a powerful quote sets the scene perfectly.

For your convenience I have created links to the Wikipedia encyclopaedia of every original author of the quote so you can add to the credibility. All quotes have been categorized under themes such as accountability, attitude, business, change, integrity, mindset and many more.

'101 Inspiring Quotes for Business and Life' includes my personal collection of favourite quotes. I have heard these quotes in workshops, speeches and in the media; I have read them in books or heard them being shared by family and friends. Every single quote in this list has, in some way, inspired me to take action or behave in a more effective way.

A Sprinkling of Magic

www.ingramcontent.com/pod-product-compliance
Lightning Source LLC
Chambersburg PA
CBHW040052160426
43192CB00002B/47